THE RO[SARY FOR] THE REST OF US

A PRACTICAL GUIDE TO OUR MOST POWERFUL PRAYER

Brent Villalobos

DEDICATION

To my wife, Barbara, who continuously reminds me of the importance of prayer and having a strong faith.

TABLE OF CONTENTS

INTRODUCTION

Every weekday I spend up to two hours in my car commuting between home and work. That is a lot of time spent staring at other cars' tail lights, billboards, and the endless gray, concrete stretch of freeway. I tried filling that time listening to music, audio books, and talk radio. But the music became repetitive, the audio books did not hold my interest for very long, and all the talk radio stressed me out. Listening to the radio is a lot like eating candy. It is fine in small doses, but consume too much and you start to feel sick. I desperately needed to find a new commuting activity. Reading, watching movies, and texting were obviously out of the question since I needed to focus on the road. But my sanity depended upon finding a more engaging and productive way of using my time in the car.

In addition to my daily commute, another frustration in my life grew larger. I always felt a sense of uneasiness that I did not pray enough throughout the day, nor did I feel deeply connected to my spiritual side. I was basically one of those once-a-week Catholics that condensed all my prayer into one hour at Sunday Mass. And even at Mass I did not focus on praying as I often daydreamed on other things such as work, finances, and my various hobbies. Here I am, a supposedly practicing Catholic, but I hardly spent any time actually practicing my faith. I knew that I should pray more but I just could not muster up the energy or get into that prayerful frame of mind during the day. Reciting prayers felt repetitive, and my mind tended to wander when I tried free-form meditation. I did not feel any closer to God or more connected with my faith. What I really needed was some way to jump-start my prayer life because spiritually I was stuck in neutral.

In August 2006 I had the fortunate opportunity of traveling to Medjugorje. It is a small village in Bosnia/Herzegovina where the Virgin Mary has allegedly appeared regularly to selected people since 1981. I am not going to dive into the details of the apparitions (I would need another book for that). These apparitions caused a spiritual boom in this village as demonstrated by pilgrims from all over the world coming there to pray. On my pilgrimage to Medjugorje I went to Mass every day, spent a considerable amount of time in front of the Blessed Sacrament in Adoration, and prayed the Stations of the Cross. This experience was so different from my usual routine of weekly Mass in that I lived in an atmosphere of persistent prayer for five straight days. Praying the rosary every day was the most important activity and the one that I looked forward to the most. Along with hundreds of other pilgrims I prayed the rosary for an hour every evening.

Praying the rosary in Medjugorje felt so peaceful and regenerative. While I prayed the rosary before, it always felt more like a race to just get through all those "Hail Mary" prayers. Perhaps it was surrounding myself with hundreds of people deep in prayer that brought me into that spiritual mood. But it finally "clicked" why the rosary is such a great prayer. It is a structured means of communicating with God. My earlier attempts at prayer and meditation did not give me the peace I felt praying in Medjugorje because those attempts were very unstructured. I said the words, but without any focus, intention, or an open heart listening to God. I was basically reciting prayers as mindless incantations. I grew frustrated that God did not speak to me. It was in Medjugorje that I realized that the reason I did not hear God was because I was not earnestly trying to talk to Him through prayer. When I learned more about the rosary and focused on the central themes of each mystery, my prayers became a dialogue with God. Not only that, but praying every day built spiritual momentum where I could build on top of the previous day's prayer and dive deeper into meditation.

Back to my frustrating daily commute. I began to think that maybe I could spend part of that time praying the rosary. Due to the rosary's simple structure I knew I could pray it while still concentrating on driving. I started praying a rosary on my morning drive to work. I thought about all the joys and courage Mary shows in the Joyful Mysteries. I meditated on how God calls me to live in the Luminous Mysteries. I asked God for strength in the face of great challenges in the Sorrowful Mysteries. And I prayed to the Holy Spirit for guidance in the Glorious Mysteries. And so my daily commute became my prayer time.

This is the part where you probably expect me to recount some great miracle that occurred as a result of my daily rosary praying. Sorry to

2

disappoint you, but I do not have a chronic illness to cure nor an estranged family member I need to forgive. Money did not come pouring into my bank account, nor did I suddenly receive a huge promotion at work. If you pray the rosary expecting great material wealth then you are setting yourself up for disappointment. The rosary is not about making you physically more comfortable in life. It is about growing deeper in your relationship with God. From all outward appearances my life has not changed for the better or worse on account of praying daily. So why do I pray the rosary? What do I gain from it?

The rosary offers me perspective on my life. I now regularly think about my relationship with God, and I focus on how He asks me to live. When you spend some quality time with God He begins to rub off on you. When I did not pray regularly, my relationship with God was more of an afterthought because I did not understand its importance. That importance grew as I began to realize that the things we tend to stress out about in life are trivial and inconsequential compared to our relationship with God. Having the nicest car, home, clothes, vacations, and stock portfolio is not what ultimately makes us happy. You only have to turn on the television to see people who have everything this world has to offer – cars, mansions, money, etc. – and yet they do not find any real happiness with that wealth as many of them turn to drugs, alcohol, and crime. That is because God, the true source of happiness, is missing in their lives.

We are not ultimately any happier even if we are lucky enough to live free of conflict, challenges, and suffering. Real happiness comes in finding the joy of living in God's grace. His grace is something that endures long after any material possession disappears. And that grace provides us the energy to endure life's inevitable challenges. And so praying the rosary gives me that perspective of knowing that God's love is all that is really important and the one true goal to have in life.

I wrote this book to offer guidance to those looking to deepen their relationship with God through the rosary. I wanted to provide some of the insights and thoughts on the rosary that I developed over the years of praying on my daily commute. Think of this book as a guide or instruction manual to the rosary. For people new to the rosary, use this book to get jump started with rosary basics. For those who already pray the rosary regularly, this book will give you some new ideas for meditations. Sometimes we all need a little jump-start to praying, whether we are getting started or trying to find a deeper level of meditation. No matter where you are in your prayer life, I hope you will find this book useful and informative and that it will help you make the most of praying the rosary.

ROSARY BASICS

Most rosaries look like a necklace (but it is not a piece of jewelry!). The first section is outside the main loop and includes the crucifix, one bead, three small beads, and another separate bead. On the crucifix, you pray the "Apostles' Creed." On the single bead next to the crucifix you pray the "Lord's Prayer" (commonly known as the "Our Father"). On each of the three smaller beads you pray a "Hail Mary." These three "Hail Mary" prayers are for the virtues of increased faith, hope, and charity. Finally, you pray the "Glory Be." The "Glory Be" does not have a bead. The last bead on the chain is where you begin praying the first of the five decades.

Physically, each decade is represented on a rosary by a separated bead followed by ten joined beads. Again, the separated bead for the first decade is actually not in the loop but is the last bead on the chain outside the main loop. On the single, separated bead you pray the "Our Father." On each of the ten joined beads you pray a "Hail Mary." At the end of each decade, you pray a "Glory Be" and the "Fatima Prayer." Note that there is no bead for those last two prayers. Many people choose to either remain holding the tenth bead of the decade or grasp that gap between that tenth bead and the one for the "Our Father" of the next decade.

After the fifth decade you pray the "Hail, Holy Queen." Many people hold that large bead or emblem of the Virgin Mary that connects the crucifix chain to the main loop. Finally, feel free to pray any extra prayers before finishing. Common prayers include the Rosary Prayer, the prayer to St. Michael, prayer for the souls in Purgatory, and any extra intentions you want to present to God.

Rosary Map: Start at the crucifix and recite the prayers listed moving counter-clockwise (it actually does not matter which direction you move). Each of the five decades consists of one "Our Father," ten "Hail Mary" prayers, one "Glory Be," and one "Fatima Prayer."

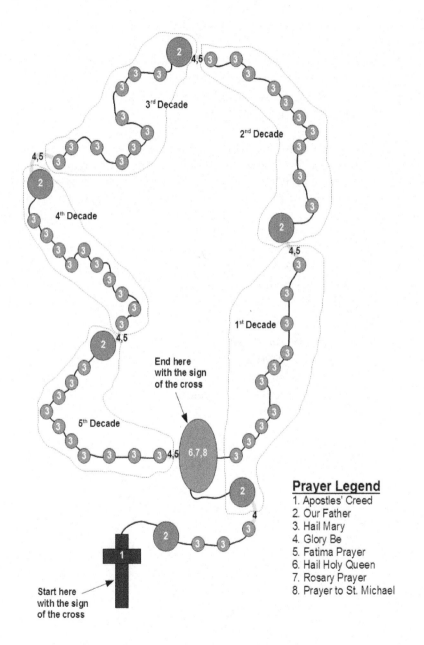

3rd Decade

2nd Decade

4,5

4th Decade

1st Decade

End here
with the sign
of the cross

5th Decade

4,5 6,7,8

4

Prayer Legend
1. Apostles' Creed
2. Our Father
3. Hail Mary
4. Glory Be
5. Fatima Prayer
6. Hail Holy Queen
7. Rosary Prayer
8. Prayer to St. Michael

Start here
with the sign
of the cross

There are 20 mysteries of the rosary divided into four groups that follow different aspects of Jesus' life. Each set of mysteries has five decades where each decade (ten joined beads and one separate bead) represents one mystery. When you pray the rosary, you typically focus on a specific set of mysteries. You typically do not mix and match mysteries from different groups. The mystery sets and their basic themes are:

- Joyful Mysteries – Jesus' birth and early childhood
- Luminous Mysteries – Jesus' ministry
- Sorrowful Mysteries – Jesus' Passion and death
- Glorious Mysteries – Jesus' Resurrection

There is a schedule for what day to pray each set of mysteries. However, it is fine to change the order or pray more than one set of mysteries on a given day. For example, perhaps you are going through a difficult time in your life and so you might want to pray the Sorrowful Mysteries more often to gather more strength. This is the schedule that Blessed Pope John Paul II suggested:

- Monday – Joyful Mysteries
- Tuesday – Sorrowful Mysteries
- Wednesday – Glorious Mysteries
- Thursday – Luminous Mysteries
- Friday – Sorrowful Mysteries
- Saturday – Joyful Mysteries
- Sunday – Glorious Mysteries (exceptions are praying the Joyful Mysteries during the Christmas season and the Sorrowful Mysteries during Lent)

PRAYERS IN THE ROSARY

You start with the "Apostles' Creed." This is similar to the "Nicene Creed" usually said after the homily during Mass. It is shorter, but the theme is the same – you profess your belief in God and the teachings of the Catholic Church. This is the first prayer of the rosary because it reminds you of your faith and helps put you in the correct frame of mind. It is important to periodically recite the basic tenants of the Catholic faith so that it will always be in your heart, mind, and actions.

"Apostles' Creed" Text
I believe in God, the Father almighty, Creator of heaven and earth, and in Jesus Christ, his only Son, our Lord, who was conceived by the Holy Spirit, born of the Virgin Mary, suffered under Pontius Pilate, was crucified, died and was buried; he descended into hell; on the third day he rose again from the dead; he ascended into heaven, and is seated at the right hand of God the Father almighty; from there he will come to judge the living and the dead. I believe in the Holy Spirit, the holy catholic Church, the communion of saints, the forgiveness of sins, the resurrection of the body, and life everlasting. Amen.

You pray the "Lord's Prayer" (commonly known as the "Our Father") before each decade. Jesus gave this prayer to His disciples when they asked Him how to pray. In this prayer you praise and give thanks to God, ask Him for forgiveness of your sins, and ask for strength to avoid sin in the future.

7

"Lord's Prayer" ("Our Father") Text
Our Father, who art in Heaven, hallowed be Thy name; Thy kingdom come; Thy will be done on earth as it is in Heaven. Give us this day our daily bread; and forgive us our trespasses as we forgive those who trespass against us; and lead us not into temptation; but deliver us from evil. Amen.

Pray the "Hail Mary" ten times in each decade. It starts with scriptural salutations to Mary and ends with a request for her prayers and intercessions. While simple in structure, this prayer is very important and powerful since you spend the most time saying it while praying the rosary. You are asking for Mary's help, guidance, and protection. She receives your prayers so make each intention count. In the rosary, you may have a specific intention each time you pray the "Hail Mary." Or you may have a single intention for the entire mystery or even the entire rosary. It is up to you how many intentions you want to present. But it is important to have intentions, thanksgivings, and remorse even if they are just generic ones (for the poor or homeless, for peace, health, etc.). Without intentions you may just go into "auto-pilot" and just say the words without actually praying for anything.

"Hail May" Text
Hail Mary, full of grace, the Lord is with thee; blessed art thou among women, and blessed is the fruit of thy womb, Jesus. Holy Mary, Mother of God, pray for us sinners, now and at the hour of our death. Amen.

It is important to remain focused while praying the rosary. The level of focus depends on your situation. Obviously you can better focus while alone in your bedroom than you can while praying in a crowded room or in your car. But just mindlessly reciting the words of a prayer while thinking about other things defeats the purpose of prayer. Imagine Jesus or Mary physically sitting next to you. Mindlessly reciting prayers would be like reading a newspaper and tuning them out while they are trying to talk to you. For the rosary to be truly effective, you really need to focus on the words and intentions behind each prayer.

The "Glory Be" is a simple, yet powerful prayer. You are expressing that God, through the Trinity, is everything. He always has been and always will be everything. By "everything" we mean that all of existence comes through God. This prayer is similar to what the Bible says about God in Revelations 22:13, "I am the Alpha and the Omega, the first and the last, the beginning and the end."

"Glory Be" Text
Glory be to the Father, and to the Son, and to the Holy Spirit. As it was in the beginning, is now, and ever shall be, world without end. Amen.

In the "Fatima Prayer" you ask Jesus for forgiveness. You acknowledge that Hell does exist and you ask Him to save you and others from that terrible fate. This is an incredibly important prayer. While other prayers focus on building up your relationship with God, this one focuses on the consequences of living in sin. Take this prayer seriously because you are literally begging God to have mercy on you and others so that you will not ultimately perish in the fires of Hell.

"Fatima Prayer" Text
O my Jesus, forgive us our sins, save us from the fires of Hell, lead all souls to Heaven, especially those who have most need of your mercy. Amen

After the fifth decade, pray the "Hail Holy Queen." Like the "Hail Mary" you ask for Mary's intersession for your petitions.

"Hail Holy Queen" Text
Hail holy queen, Mother of Mercy, our life, our sweetness and our hope! To thee do we cry, poor banished children of Eve; to thee do we send up our sighs, mourning and weeping in this valley of tears. Turn then, most gracious advocate, thine eyes of mercy toward us, and after this our exile, show unto us the blessed fruit of thy womb, Jesus. O clement, O loving, O sweet Virgin Mary! Pray for us, O Holy Mother of God, that we may be made worthy of the promises of Christ. Amen.

There are many other prayers recited at the end of the rosary that are not technically part of the rosary. But there is no harm in spending a few extra minutes in prayer after completing the rosary. One such prayer, just called the "Rosary Prayer," is often said after the "Hail Holy Queen." In the "Rosary Prayer" you ask the Virgin Mary for help living what each mystery teaches and for increased faith that God hears your intentions. This prayer really ties up a rosary meditation session nicely. It makes you realize that prayer does not end once you put the rosary down, but is something you carry with you throughout the day. All your intentions, promises, concerns, and thanksgivings that you present to God in the rosary should always be on your heart and reflected in your actions.

"Rosary Prayer" Text
O God, whose only begotten Son, by His life, death, and resurrection, has purchased for us the rewards of eternal salvation. Grant, we beseech Thee, that while meditating on these mysteries of the most holy Rosary of the Blessed Virgin Mary, that we may both imitate what they contain and obtain what they promise, through Christ our Lord. Amen.

Another great closing prayer is the prayer to St. Michael. In this prayer you ask him for protection against Satan. It is important to realize that there is evil in this world brought forth by Satan and his minions. You pray the rosary, in part, to protect yourself against evil influences. Part of avoiding sin is recognizing that evil does exist in this world and to ask the angels for help against this wicked, yet powerful, force. There is no better protector than St. Michael the Archangel, who is the patron saint of police and soldiers and is often represented holding down Satan with his boot.

"Prayer to Saint Michael" Text
Saint Michael the Archangel, defend us in battle. Be our protection against the wickedness and snares of the devil. May God rebuke him, we humbly pray; and do Thou, O Prince of the Heavenly Host - by the Divine Power of God - cast into Hell, Satan and all the evil spirits, who roam throughout the world seeking the ruin of souls. Amen.

Another popular prayer is praying for the souls in Purgatory. Purgatory is an intermediate place for those souls that are bound for Heaven but still have to be purified of the damaging effects of their sins. Remember, the souls in Purgatory can no longer pray for themselves and are completely dependent on God's mercy and your prayers for them. This is a good time to remember and pray for your ancestors and the recently departed as many of them might require your prayers to find eternal rest. There are many Purgatory prayers. Jesus gave this one to St. Gertrude the Great where He promised to release many souls from Purgatory each time we pray it.

"St. Gertrude's Prayer for Souls in Purgatory" Text
Eternal Father, I offer Thee the Most Precious Blood of Thy Divine Son, Jesus, in union with the Masses said throughout the world today, for all the holy souls in Purgatory, for sinners everywhere, for sinners in the universal church, those in my own home and within my family. Amen.

INTEGRATING THE ROSARY INTO YOUR LIFE

One hurdle people have praying the rosary is that they think they need to dedicate a huge chunk of time to it. While it is best to pray all five decades of a rosary uninterrupted to dive deeper into meditation, many people do not have that luxury in their schedule. But there are many places to squeeze in time to pray a decade or two throughout the day. Someone can usually pray a decade in about four or five minutes. Think about your daily routine and where you can find five minutes here and five minutes there. Many of you will find that you do have the time to pray five decades of a rosary every day. Here are a few times you can squeeze in some prayers throughout the day:

- Taking a shower in the morning
- Commuting (drivers, be sure to still pay attention to the road)
- On a lunch break
- Doing laundry or folding clothes
- Exercising (or while taking a break from exercise)
- Before getting out of your car after parking somewhere
- Waiting for a movie to start
- Right after dinner
- Before going to bed
- During a TV commercial break
- Instead of watching a TV show
- Explicitly make time in your schedule
- Instead of browsing the internet

Some of these times allow for better quality prayer than others. For example, I usually pray while driving to work. That means my attention is split between praying and driving. It is not an even split as I usually focus more on the road for obvious safety reasons. But this time works well for me as I am free of other interruptions such as phone calls, emails, and meetings. Someone who prays before bed in a quiet room probably has much more focus than someone trying to squeeze in a few "Hail Mary" prayers during a commercial break while watching TV. But any amount of prayer is better than no prayer at all. The idea is to make praying part of your daily routine.

> **Words to Live By:**
> "The Rosary is the most beautiful and richest of all prayers to the Mediatrix of all grace; it is the prayer that touches most the heart of the Mother of God. Say it each day." (Pope Saint Pius X)

Praying the rosary is a lot like exercise; you make gains in small pieces. Someone cannot go from no exercise at all to running a marathon in one day. Furthermore, those who exercise regularly probably do not notice the small, incremental improvements in their health after each workout.

The same ideas that apply to exercise apply to praying the rosary. You will probably not pray a rosary mystery and suddenly feel completely happy and at peace. But over time you will start to see life differently. Maybe you will not stress over things that ultimately are not very important in the long run. Maybe you will have better focus on those things that are more important such as living God's will. Hopefully you will be more influenced by the Holy Spirit and avoid the temptation to sin.

Do not give up praying the rosary after a day or two just because you do not see immediate results. Remember, the goal of prayer is to realize God's plan for you, integrate it into your life, and eventually find eternal happiness in Heaven. That means that you have an entire lifetime to practice praying. Do not worry if you do not feel any different at the start. In fact, you may not feel any different in a few weeks, months, or even years. God works with each of us differently and some of us may have to walk down a longer road to eventually come into His grace (more on this theme in the Fourth Joyful Mystery). Remember, God works in mysterious ways, and sometimes He transforms us so subtly we do not even realize how we changed over time.

It is important that you pray the rosary earnestly. If this is your first time praying the rosary regularly then please set aside some time so you can really concentrate. Going back to the exercise analogy, you cannot expect to get into great shape physically by working out halfheartedly.

You cannot do one poorly-formed pushup once a week and eat junk food and expect to be in super shape. Similarly, you need to develop good form for praying the rosary, especially in the beginning. Starting anything new and different can be a challenge initially. Think of praying the rosary as spiritual boot camp where you need to put in a lot of effort up front to give your spiritual life a jolt. But once you find your rhythm, the benefits of prayer really start to multiply. Once you are comfortable praying the rosary then it becomes much easier to integrate it throughout the day if you like.

Words to Live By:
"The Rosary is the most excellent form of prayer and the most efficacious means of attaining eternal life. It is the remedy for all our evils, the root of all our blessings. There is no more excellent way of praying." (Pope Leo XIII)

There are several ways to pray the rosary – alone, with a partner, or as a group. Each method has its pros and cons. Praying alone has the advantage that you can pray at your own pace. For example, when you pray alone you can take a break in the middle of the rosary to further meditate or say a special intention. Or if you start to feel like you are just rushing through the prayers without a lot of thought and concentration, you can take a break and resume when you are more focused. You do not typically have that option when you pray with other people.

Praying alone also allows you to choose the time and place. Without needing to coordinate with others, you can pray when and where you feel you will be best able to focus. If you are a morning person, then perhaps praying after you get up is a good option. Other people like to pray at night after the day has settled down. However, this increased flexibility also carries increased responsibility. Without finding a good time and place to pray the rosary you might end up never praying it at all as you tend to just put it off every day. The best idea is to find the environment that works best for you and then try to stick to it. If you have to, add rosary time to your schedule and set reminders. Like exercise, sometimes the hardest part of praying is just getting started and finding that rhythm.

Instead of praying alone you can also find a prayer partner. This could be a spouse, family member, or good friend. An advantage to this approach is that you have someone else to motivate you to pray. Your rosary partner might provide that little burst of motivation to get started praying when you otherwise may have skipped it if you prayed alone. Much like how people trying to lose weight or stop smoking often do better when they have a partner at their side, sometimes we also need that little kick to our prayer life.

A prayer partner also provides intentions and insights that you may not think of when you pray by yourself. Maybe your partner has some very special intentions that need more prayers. Even if your partner's intention is very general, such as, "pray for the sick," you might have a more specific intention in your heart. Regardless, both of you will be praying for that intention even if it is not spoken. Many people find it comforting to share their intentions with others and know that many people are praying for them even when they are not specifically voiced.

You can also try to form or join a prayer group. Think of it like a book club except that people come together to pray. This has many of the same advantages as having a prayer partner, only multiplied. There are many more intentions to pray for with multiple people. If people are not comfortable saying their intentions you can set up a system where people write out intentions on a piece of paper before you start praying the rosary. And then, before each decade, you read those intentions out loud.

A rosary group can also bring a social aspect to prayer and sharing your faith. Perhaps you can form a weekly rosary where you pray at a different home each time. Maybe you will want to make it a pot luck and ask people to bring food to eat after you finish praying. Many parishes and other religious organizations have rosary groups that meet regularly that you can join. If your parish does not have one then you can always ask to start it. All it takes is a few people and a place to meet. It is amazing how fast it can grow from that small beginning.

While it is nice to pray with many people, one disadvantage is that you may not find that calm, meditative environment you would otherwise find praying alone. You are now at the mercy of the pace of the group, which usually means you cannot pause if you want to say a few extra prayers for a special intention or if you just need to take a short break. When praying with others you might have a tendency to just go into auto-pilot and say the words without really focusing on the prayers. Some people find praying with other people distracting. Of course, there is no rule saying that you can only choose one way of praying the rosary. You can join a rosary group that meets weekly or monthly and pray alone the other times.

There are other prayers you can add to the rosary when you are in a group. As stated earlier, the group can pray for different intentions that each member either says before each decade or writes down ahead of time. You can also begin or end each decade with a verse from the Bible (this is known as praying a scriptural rosary). While many people choose passages that are relevant to the mystery being prayed, there is nothing wrong with using different passages so that people do not become complacent by hearing the same verses every time. If the group feels really adventurous, try singing hymns as well.

While rosary groups have a social element to them, remember to keep the focus on prayer. The praying should come before any eating, drinking, and socializing. After all, who can focus and pray when they are in a food coma? There is an ancient Chinese proverb that states, "Full stomach, empty head." The same thing can be said about prayer. If you party and socialize before praying then you will not have a lot of energy left for prayer. The rosary should be the focus, not the afterthought.

There are some important rules to keep in mind when attending rosary prayer groups. Remember, rosary groups are a little different from other social gatherings. Keep these in mind:

- Be on time. It is distracting to others when the doorbell rings when the group is in the middle of prayer. If you are going to be late, let the host know ahead of time and try to arrange a way you can arrive without distracting the group.
- Do not leave early. Similar to being late, leaving early can also be a distraction.
- Bring your own rosary. Most people do not have a lot of spare rosaries lying around.
- Move at the pace of the group. While the group may move slower or faster than you are used to, you just have to go with the flow. You can pray at your own pace later when you are alone.

Whether alone, with a partner, or in a group, praying the rosary will be more meaningful when you make the effort to integrate it into your daily life.

OBLIGATIONS AND BENEFITS OF THE ROSARY

Roman Catholic tradition on the power of the rosary states that through Saint Dominic, founder of the Dominican order in 1217, and through Blessed Alan de Rupe, the Blessed Virgin Mary made fifteen specific promises to Christians who pray the rosary. Both men were devoted to the rosary. One of the cornerstones of the Dominican order is praying and spreading the devotion of the rosary. Although Saint Dominic was a faithful believer in the power of the rosary, devotion of the rosary slowly started to fade over time. In 1460, Alan de Rupe, also a Dominican, restored devotion to the rosary. He founded The Confraternities of the Rosary which still exists today and which anyone can join (see http://www.rosary-center.org).

The Virgin Mary made the following promises to Saint Dominic and Blessed Alan de Rupe for those who routinely pray the rosary. According to the Confraternities of the Rosary website, "routinely" means praying all mysteries at least once a week. Mary's promises are:

1. Whoever shall faithfully serve me by the recitation of the rosary, shall receive signal graces.

2. I promise my special protection and the greatest graces to all those who shall recite the rosary.

3. The rosary shall be a powerful armor against Hell. It will destroy vice, decrease sin, and defeat heresies.

4. It will cause virtue and good works to flourish; it will obtain for souls the abundant mercy of God; it will withdraw the heart of men from the love of the world and its vanities, and will lift them to the

desire of eternal things. Oh, that souls would sanctify themselves by this means.

5. The soul which recommends itself to me by the recitation of the rosary shall not perish.

6. Whoever shall recite the rosary devoutly, applying himself to the consideration of its sacred mysteries, shall never be conquered by misfortune. God will not chastise him in His justice, he shall not by an unprovided death; if he be just he shall remain in the grace of God, and become worthy of eternal life.

7. Whoever shall have a true devotion for the rosary shall not die without the sacraments of the Church.

8. Those who are faithful to recite the rosary shall have during their life and at their death the light of God and the plenitude of His graces; at the moment of death they shall participate in the merits of the saints in paradise.

9. I shall deliver from Purgatory those who have been devoted to the rosary.

10. The faithful children of the rosary shall merit a high degree of glory in Heaven.

11. You shall obtain all you ask of me by the recitation of the rosary.

12. All those who propagate the holy rosary shall be aided by me in their necessities.

13. I have obtained from my Divine Son that all the advocates of the rosary shall have for intercessors the entire celestial court during their life and at the hour of death.

14. All who recite the rosary are my son, and brothers of my only son Jesus Christ.

15. Devotion of my rosary is a great sign of predestination.

Keep in mind that these promises are contingent upon avoiding sin. You cannot sin to your heart's content and then expect to remain in God's grace by praying the rosary. If you treat the rosary as some sort of "get out of jail free" card then you really are not understanding the main point of the rosary. It is not some magic spell that you chant that automatically grants you a spot in Heaven. Praying the rosary is not about uttering simple phrases, but attempting to build a relationship with God. If you are not trying to open a dialog with God through the rosary then you really are not earnestly praying it. And if your heart is set on committing sins, then you really are not letting God into your heart and listening to His guidance.

Think of the rosary as a road map that will guide you into God's heavenly kingdom. It helps show you how to live in God's grace, but it is ultimately up to you whether you want to follow the path that God lays before you. Look again at the first promise. Mary said that you will receive signal graces. A signal grace is a sign from God to help us make the right decisions in life. These signs may not come from a burning bush or a booming voice from the sky. A sign might be as subtle as an awakening of conscience when you choose to do the right thing when you otherwise would have sinned. Many times we receive benefits from praying the rosary without even knowing it.

Another important aspect of these promises is that Mary does not promise that praying the rosary will cause all of life's problems to disappear. Again, the rosary is not some sort of lucky charm that protects you from misfortune. As you continue to pray the rosary you will begin to understand that when Mary speaks of "obtaining all that you ask" (promise #11) she is not talking about the trivial things that we think are so important. If you pray the rosary hoping to win the lottery then you really are not understanding the meaning of the rosary. You might even pray for a miracle such as God curing a loved one of a disease. And while that is certainly a great thing to pray for, being physically cured of some illness does not ultimately have any impact on the health of your soul. Do not think of the rosary as something that will protect you from physical harm and inconvenience. Rather, think of it as providing guidance and strength in the face of life's difficult moments.

The relatively small amount of time spent praying the rosary yields tremendous results. Think about all those exercise infomercials on television. They promise you will be healthier, stronger, and more attractive. All you have to do is use their product 30 minutes a day. People spend millions of dollars on exercise equipment, programs, and supplements. Yet very few see the benefits. But look at the promises Mary makes for those who pray the rosary. You can receive God's grace, defense against sin and temptation, reduced time in Purgatory, and eternal life in the glory of Heaven. All you need to do to receive these benefits is dedicate 20-30 minutes of your day to praying the rosary. A few minutes a day for the rosary can translate to an eternity of joy and happiness in Heaven. Now that sounds like a great deal!

18

HOW TO USE THIS BOOK

This book offers thoughts and ideas for rosary meditation. You should read this book in addition to praying the rosary. This is not a novel or research paper. Think of it more as a guidebook. It is a middle ground between giving a few words on the rosary and providing an entire encyclical. It has enough commentary to get your mind focused on the central themes of each rosary mystery, but not bog you down with a lot of heavy theology and Church doctrine. This book is not about detailing the Biblical, historical, and theological roots of each rosary mystery. Instead, this book will act as a map to help guide you in your prayers.

Remember, the most important aspect of praying the rosary is what you present to God, not just reciting verbatim prayers or what you read in a book. This book gives you a starting point for rosary meditation and allows you to fill in your prayers with your own intentions, concerns, and thanksgivings.

The rosary is more than just recitation of standard prayers. It is divided into mysteries for a reason. Each mystery has a central theme on which you can meditate. Focus on the theme behind each mystery and what it might say about your relationship with God, with His Church, and with others.

There are several ways you can read this book. It all depends on your style of praying. If you are new to praying the rosary or do not already have a preferred style, give each strategy a try to see which one suits you best.

1. **Read the book straight through.** This strategy works if you want an overview of the rosary and the general theme of each mystery. You probably will not remember the specifics of each mystery meditation when you do pray the rosary, but perhaps a few central ideas will remain in your mind. It is a good idea for everyone to read this book straight through at least once to learn how all the mysteries connect together.
2. **Read the meditation for all five decades before praying a rosary.** Think of reading all the meditations for all mysteries as a warm up before diving into praying the rosary. Maybe you will remember some specific word or phrase from this text while you are praying that will help you dive deeper into meditation. This is also a good strategy if you do not want to interrupt your praying with reading.
3. **Read the meditation before praying each mystery.** The meditation will stay fresh in your mind as you pray each decade and will make you less likely to lose your concentration while reciting the prayers. This method is particularly helpful if you do not have any specific meditation for a decade or have problems finding a central theme. Do not use this strategy if you do not like to split your meditation time between saying the set of prayers in each decade and reading text.

Words to Live By:
"The Rosary is a powerful weapon to put the demons to flight and to keep oneself from sin...If you desire peace in your hearts, in your homes, and in your country, assemble each evening to recite the Rosary. Let not even one day pass without saying it, no matter how burdened you may be with many cares and labors." (Pope Pius XI)

You should also reread this book as you grow in your prayer life. Passages in this book may have a different meaning to you as you dive deeper into the rosary. As your situation in life changes, so might your interpretation of different rosary mysteries. You will see the mysteries and these meditations in a different light as you have new experiences in your personal, professional, and spiritual life.

Each decade in this book starts with a passage from a Gospel. Reading the Gospel passage, either in full before each decade or between each "Hail Mary," is a good way to stay focused on the central messages of each mystery. Weaving Biblical verses between the standard prayers is known as the scriptural rosary.

Each decade in this book ends with intentions that focus around the theme of each mystery. You can read them at the beginning of the decade or weave them between the "Hail Mary" prayers. If you find yourself switching into auto-pilot while praying, reading the intentions is a good way to refocus on your meditations. While most of the intentions are general, perhaps they will remind you of specific people who need your prayers.

The artwork in this book also aids to keep you focused during the meditation and prayer. If you are easily distracted, viewing religious imagery can really help you get back into the right frame of mind. As they say, "A picture is worth a thousand words." Often great works of art can speak to people at a deeper level than words. As you pray each mystery, look at the images and let them inspire you. Imagine yourself as an observer in those pictures of Mary or Jesus Christ. What would you tell Jesus if you were present during those depicted moments? What do you think He would tell you?

Words to Live By:
"Among all the devotions approved by the Church none has been so favored by so many miracles as the devotion of the Most Holy Rosary." (Pope Pius IX)

THE JOYFUL MYSTERIES

The Annunciation
The Visitation
The Nativity
The Presentation in the Temple
The Finding of Jesus in the Temple

The Joyful Mysteries focus on Mary accepting God's plan and Jesus' early childhood. We pray with great joy that God so loved us that He humbled Himself by becoming man so that we may know Him better.

THE FIRST JOYFUL MYSTERY
THE ANNUNCIATION

[26]In the sixth month, the angel Gabriel was sent from God to a town of Galilee called Nazareth, [27]to a virgin betrothed to a man named Joseph, of the house of David, and the virgin's name was Mary. [28]And coming to her, he said, "Hail, favored one! The Lord is with you."

[29]But she was greatly troubled at what was said and pondered what sort of greeting this might be. [30]Then the angel said to her, "Do not be afraid, Mary, for you have found favor with God. [31]Behold, you will conceive in your womb and bear a son, and you shall name him Jesus. [32]He will be great and will be called Son of the Most High, and the Lord God will give him the throne of David his father, [33]and he will rule over the house of Jacob forever, and of his kingdom there will be no end."

[34]But Mary said to the angel, "How can this be, since I have no relations with a man?"

[35]And the angel said to her in reply, "The holy Spirit will come upon you, and the power of the Most High will overshadow you. Therefore the child to be born will be called holy, the Son of God. [36]And behold, Elizabeth, your relative, has also conceived a son in her old age, and this is the sixth month for her who was called barren; [37]for nothing will be impossible for God."

[38]Mary said, "Behold, I am the handmaid of the Lord. May it be done to me according to your word." Then the angel departed from her.

Luke 1:26-38

In the Annunciation the angel Gabriel asked Mary, a mere teenager, to be the Mother of God. As you pray this mystery think about how you would react to such a request. What would you do if you found out that God chose you to bring His son into this world? Would you run outside rejoicing as if you just won the lottery? Would you turn weak and pale, pass out, and then hope that it was all just a dream? Would you calmly tell the angel Gabriel that you are not ready and there are others who would make a better choice?

Fortunately for us, God has only asked one person in the history of the world to be the mother of Jesus Christ, so that is not something He will likely ask of us. When compared to our Mother Mary, God asks relatively little of us. God does not ask us to sacrifice our son as He asked Abraham. Nor does He ask us to act like Moses and stand up to a pharaoh, demanding that he release his slaves. But we often fall short of living up to our relatively small responsibilities such as attending Sunday Mass, receiving the Sacrament of Reconciliation, or just taking a few minutes out of our day for prayer.

The Annunciation by Paolo de Matteis (1712)

When we fail to make time for God in our lives we are not preparing ourselves to follow the path He lays before us.

Why are we unprepared for the times when God asks something of us? He asks us to follow His laws faithfully and put Him first in our lives. How does God make this request? God speaks to us every day through the Pope, the Church's teachings, our priests, the Bible, saints, and angels with the message to follow Him and do His will. And yet we so often ignore God's messengers. Or we hear His message and willfully choose to ignore it because it sounds too difficult or conflicts with how we want to live. When He asks us to follow Him, do we tell Him, "not now" and to ask us at a more convenient time? Or do we tell Him a resounding "YES!" only to follow another road besides the one He lays before us? God asks us to follow Him more times than we realize, but we often tell Him "no" through our words, thoughts, and actions.

When we pray this mystery may we recognize that God calls us every day to follow Him. Let us imitate Mary in the Annunciation and tell God we will follow Him wherever He leads us. Mary put her faith in God knowing that He never gives us more than we can handle. We should put our faith in His plan knowing that it is the only true path to eternal happiness. The Holy Spirit purified and strengthened Mary to carry the large responsibility of bringing Jesus Christ into this world. That same Holy Spirit strengthens us today to accept God's will in our own lives. With the Holy Spirit, the Church, and Mary as our guides we are adequately prepared to follow His path. Let us pray that when God asks us to follow Him we can confidently say as Mary did, "*May it be done to me according to your word*" (Luke 1:38).

Intentions for this Mystery:
- For vocations, that we all accept God's plan for us.
- For mothers, that they have the strength to instill God's Word in their children.
- For those who reject God's plan, that the Holy Spirit will lead them back to His truth.
- That we have faith in God's plan for us that it will lead us to eternal happiness in Heaven.
- For those who are persecuted and struggle in life because they try to live according to God's will. May they be comforted knowing that they imitate Mary in the Annunciation by accepting the path God lays before them.

The Annunciation by William Brassey Hole (20th century)

THE SECOND JOYFUL MYSTERY
THE VISITATION

³⁹During those days Mary set out and traveled to the hill country in haste to a town of Judah, ⁴⁰where she entered the house of Zechariah and greeted Elizabeth. ⁴¹When Elizabeth heard Mary's greeting, the infant leaped in her womb, and Elizabeth, filled with the holy Spirit, ⁴²cried out in a loud voice and said, "Most blessed are you among women, and blessed is the fruit of your womb. ⁴³And how does this happen to me, that the mother of my Lord should come to me? ⁴⁴For at the moment the sound of your greeting reached my ears, the infant in my womb leaped for joy. ⁴⁵Blessed are you who believed that what was spoken to you by the Lord would be fulfilled."

⁴⁶And Mary said: "My soul proclaims the greatness of the Lord; my spirit rejoices in God my savior. ⁴⁸For he has looked upon his handmaid's lowliness; behold, from now on will all ages call me blessed. ⁴⁹The Mighty One has done great things for me, and holy is his name. ⁵⁰His mercy is from age to age to those who fear him. ⁵¹He has shown might with his arm, dispersed the arrogant of mind and heart. ⁵²He has thrown down the rulers from their thrones but lifted up the lowly. ⁵³The hungry he has filled with good things; the rich he has sent away empty. ⁵⁴He has helped Israel his servant, remembering his mercy, ⁵⁵according to his promise to our fathers, to Abraham and to his descendants forever."

⁵⁶Mary remained with her about three months and then returned to her home.

Luke 1:39-56

This mystery of the Visitation is a great example of using God's grace to help others. Traveling in the time of the Roman Empire was no easy task. It would take weeks, if not months, to travel between villages. It was challenging and dangerous for even the strongest traveler, let alone a pregnant girl. Despite the hardship, Mary made the journey to share the good news with her cousin and help in any way she could. As the Mother of God she chose to use God's grace to serve others instead of expecting others to serve her. As Mary said in Luke's Gospel, God's greatness is found in His lowly servants doing His will. We see this same theme through Jesus, King of Heaven, who came into this world as a humble servant. Like His mother, Jesus came to serve others and not to be served.

Visitazione by Matteo Rosselli (17th century)

The Mystery of the Visitation reminds us about the difference between receiving God's grace and using it by practicing good works. We receive God's grace by praying, fasting, and receiving the sacraments (such as washing away sin during Confession). But do we use the gift of grace to help others in need, or do we keep it bottled up inside? For example, can you give more time for charitable works? Or do you have a friend or family member who needs your help? Just because someone may not ask you for help does not mean they do not need it. There are opportunities to put God's grace into practice all around us. Are we using that grace to its full potential or are we letting it go to waste by hoarding it?

The lesson behind the Visitation is that God calls us to put His grace into action. It is true that our faith is something that is deeply personal. But it is also something that should be very public. God gives us grace not only for our own sake, but to also help others in their conversion towards God's truth and their ultimate salvation. Remember the old saying, "Actions speak louder than words." Let us remember that about prayer. Let us not just pay lip service to God, but actually put into action what we believe and profess. Prayer is good and necessary, but it forms the foundation for good works and is not solely an end in itself.

Imagine Elizabeth's surprise when she found herself pregnant although she was barren. Many people find themselves in Elizabeth's situation when God gives them an unexpected surprise. It might be an unexpected pregnancy or some other life-altering challenge. However, God also puts people in our lives to help face these difficulties. In this mystery, God put Mary in Elizabeth's life during her pregnancy. We should pray that we can see and accept the help others might offer us during our difficult times instead of feeling like we need to face them alone. Furthermore, we should remember to act like Mary and have the awareness and energy to help those in need all around us. God placed us in this world, at this particular time, and with specific abilities for a reason. Are you using God's grace to the best of your God-given abilities to help those in need whether it be a family member, friend, coworker, or even a complete stranger?

Intentions for this Mystery:
- That we may live our faith fully every day.
- For strength to spread God's Word through words and actions.
- That we are aware of those less fortunate and find the strength and compassion to reach out to them.
- For priests everywhere, that they faithfully spread the Word of God.
- For those who hide their faith, that they may find the strength to live it publicly.
- For expectant mothers and fathers, that they realize that their unborn baby is a gift from God.

Visitación by Jerónimo Cosida (16th century)

THE THIRD JOYFUL MYSTERY
THE NATIVITY

⁴And Joseph too went up from Galilee from the town of Nazareth to Judea, to the city of David that is called Bethlehem, because he was of the house and family of David, ⁵to be enrolled with Mary, his betrothed, who was with child.

⁶While they were there, the time came for her to have her child, ⁷and she gave birth to her firstborn son. She wrapped him in swaddling clothes and laid him in a manger, because there was no room for them in the inn.

⁸Now there were shepherds in that region living in the fields and keeping the night watch over their flock. ⁹The angel of the Lord appeared to them and the glory of the Lord shone around them, and they were struck with great fear. ¹⁰The angel said to them, "Do not be afraid; for behold, I proclaim to you good news of great joy that will be for all the people. ¹¹For today in the city of David a savior has been born for you who is Messiah and Lord.

¹⁶So they went in haste and found Mary and Joseph, and the infant lying in the manger. ¹⁷When they saw this, they made known the message that had been told them about this child. ¹⁸All who heard it were amazed by what had been told them by the shepherds. ¹⁹And Mary kept all these things, reflecting on them in her heart. ²⁰Then the shepherds returned, glorifying and praising God for all they had heard and seen, just as it had been told to them.

Luke 2:4-11, 16-20

In the Nativity we reflect and pray on Jesus' humble birth in a stable. This is an important mystery, not just during the Christmas season, but throughout the year. The nature of Jesus' humble birth provides a foundation for His teachings and gives us a clear picture on how Jesus calls us to live.

Humility is one of the main themes of this mystery. Jesus came into this world in the humblest of surroundings. Hundreds of miles away from Rome, the seat of power in the world, Mary gave birth to the true King of Kings. Jesus was born without money, riches, or any earthly power. He was born surrounded by peasant shepherds, not a royal court. This humble birth was no accident as it showed from the beginning of Jesus' life that His ways were not the world's ways. His mission was not one of earthly conquest and accumulation of

Illustration by O.A. Stemler (1925)

power, nor was it to bring the Jews out of Roman occupation. Instead, He showed us that living a humble life as God's servant was His way and the only path to His heavenly kingdom.

Jesus' humble birth contrasts sharply with how modern society celebrates Christmas. Christmas is typically a time of extravagance and consumerism. It is a time when we focus on gifts and other trappings. The word *trappings* means some sort of decoration or fancy outward appearance. We see the trappings of Christmas everywhere during the holiday season such as in the amount of money spent on presents, decorations, clothes, and food. But it is not only Christmas when we seem to put a premium on the trappings of life. Many of us focus every day on owning expensive clothes, buying the largest television, owning the fanciest car, and do everything we can (both ethically and unethically) to accumulate as much wealth as possible. While trying to earn a comfortable living is not inherently bad, when we start to put the comforts of this world above the rewards of the next we move away from how Jesus calls us to live. The trappings of this life literally trap us into living only for this world which amounts to absolutely nothing in Jesus' heavenly kingdom.

Let us pray that we have the strength to live as Jesus did — humbly and meekly. Let us pray for the strength to resist putting our earthly desires ahead of our heavenly needs. In the end God will not judge us based on the cars we drive, the value of our stock portfolio, or what position we held at our jobs. Those are just the trappings of this world, the ornamental decorations. How well we follow Jesus' path is the real substance. Let us pray and meditate on this mystery that we might embrace Jesus' humble ways as manifested in the Nativity.

Intentions for this Mystery:
- For Church and world leaders, that they may use their power in humble service to Jesus.
- For parents, that they teach their children the power of living for Jesus' kingdom.
- That everyone shares what God has given them with the less fortunate.
- That we remember and embrace Jesus as our Savior all year round.
- That we accept Jesus' teachings for what they are and not try to transform them to suit our desires.

The Nativity by Cuzco School (1725-1775)

THE FOURTH JOYFUL MYSTERY
THE PRESENTATION

^{22}When the days were completed for their purification according to the law of Moses, they took him up to Jerusalem to present him to the Lord, ^{23}just as it is written in the law of the Lord, "Every male that opens the womb shall be consecrated to the Lord," ^{24}and to offer the sacrifice of "a pair of turtledoves or two young pigeons," in accordance with the dictate in the law of the Lord.

^{25}Now there was a man in Jerusalem whose name was Simeon. This man was righteous and devout, awaiting the consolation of Israel, and the holy Spirit was upon him. ^{26}It had been revealed to him by the holy Spirit that he should not see death before he had seen the Messiah of the Lord. ^{27}He came in the Spirit into the temple; and when the parents brought in the child Jesus to perform the custom of the law in regard to him, ^{28}he took him into his arms and blessed God, saying: ^{29}"Now, Master, you may let your servant go in peace, according to your word,^{30}for my eyes have seen your salvation, ^{31}which you prepared in sight of all the peoples, ^{32}a light for revelation to the Gentiles, and glory for your people Israel."

^{33}The child's father and mother were amazed at what was said about him; ^{34}and Simeon blessed them and said to Mary his mother, "Behold, this child is destined for the fall and rise of many in Israel, and to be a sign that will be contradicted ^{35}(and you yourself a sword will pierce) so that the thoughts of many hearts may be revealed."

Luke 2:22-35

In this mystery we see Mary and Joseph present Jesus at the temple, as was the Jewish tradition. They encountered a man named Simeon whom the Holy Spirit said would not experience death until he had seen the Anointed One. Upon seeing Jesus, Simeon said *"Now, Master, you may let your servant go in peace, according to your word"* (Luke 2:29). Simeon is an example of how our faith requires patience, endurance, and moral fortitude. While there are times when we may not feel God's presence in our lives, our faith tells us that He is always near and always hears our prayers.

It is a common occurrence for people to feel discouraged because they do not feel close to Jesus. They often talk about how they pray, go to Mass, fast, and read the Bible, and yet do not feel the Lord's grace. We can all look to Simeon as an example of how even the most just and pious people need to show patience and have faith that the Lord will present Himself in the way that will ultimately lead us to Him. It would not have surprised anyone if Simeon had given up waiting in the temple for the Anointed One after many fruitless years. But in the end God rewarded him for his persistence and faith. Similarly, if we can hang on and remain faithful, even

Simeon the Righteous by Alexey Yegorov (19th century)

when it seems like God does not hear our prayers or notice our good deeds, He will reward us with the eternal happiness of Heaven.

Why must our faith be so difficult to live at times? Why do we not receive direct answers to our prayers from a thundering voice in the clouds like so many people in the Bible? Why must we endure such hardship and struggle even when we do our best to live according to Jesus' teachings? Hardship is God's way of making sure we grow strong in our faith. A plant or a small tree must develop deep roots to survive in a harsh climate. Similarly, our faith grows stronger when we desire to remain close to God in the face of life's challenges. Without the trials and tribulations we would become lazy, complacent, and spiritually weak, making us prime targets for Satan and his minions. God does not want any of us to come under Satan's control, and that is why He gives us the opportunity to build spiritual strength by remaining faithful to Him regardless of the circumstances.

When we meditate on the Fourth Joyful Mystery let us remember Simeon and how his faith and patience were ultimately rewarded. We must pray for those who have fallen on the long and difficult road of faith, that they get back up and have the strength to live as Jesus calls them. Remember, God has a plan for each of us, and that plan will ultimately lead us to His heavenly kingdom. We just need to allow the Holy Spirit to guide us, especially in those times when it feels like God is the most distant from us. It is those times of great hardship when Jesus presents Himself to us, although maybe not in the way we expect. Remember in your prayers to not only speak to Jesus but also allow Him to respond, for He will show you the way to Him.

Intentions for this Mystery:
- For patience with God's plan for us.
- For those who have left the Church because they do not feel God in their lives, that they may return with renewed strength and endurance to live according to His will.
- For those who are persecuted for living their faith, that they remain strong in their convictions.
- That we all find the strength and endurance to continue looking for Jesus in our lives.
- For those who minister to the poor and sick, that they stay strong despite their continuous encounters with suffering.

Presentazione di Gesù al Tempio by
Guercino (1623)

THE FIFTH JOYFUL MYSTERY
THE FINDING OF JESUS IN THE TEMPLE

⁴¹Each year his parents went to Jerusalem for the feast of Passover, ⁴²and when he was twelve years old, they went up according to festival custom. ⁴³After they had completed its days, as they were returning,. the boy Jesus remained behind in Jerusalem, but his parents did not know it. ⁴⁴Thinking that he was in the caravan, they journeyed for a day and looked for him among their relatives and acquaintances, ⁴⁵but not finding him, they returned to Jerusalem to look for him.

⁴⁶After three days they found him in the temple, sitting in the midst of the teachers, listening to them and asking them questions, ⁴⁷and all who heard him were astounded at his understanding and his answers. ⁴⁸When his parents saw him, they were astonished, and his mother said to him, "Son, why have you done this to us? Your father and I have been looking for you with great anxiety."

⁴⁹And he said to them, "Why were you looking for me? Did you not know that I must be in my Father's house?"

⁵⁰But they did not understand what he said to them. ⁵¹He went down with them and came to Nazareth, and was obedient to them; and his mother kept all these things in her heart. ⁵²And Jesus advanced [in] wisdom and age and favor before God and man.

Luke 2:41-52

When returning from a festival in Jerusalem, Mary and Joseph noticed that Jesus was not in their caravan. They went back to Jerusalem and searched for Jesus for three days before finding Him in the temple talking to the elders. When Mary said that she and Joseph had been searching for Him in sorrow, Jesus responded, *"Why were you looking for me? Did you not know that I must be in my Father's house?"* (Luke 2:49).

Mary and Joseph traveled for a day before noticing that Jesus was missing from the caravan. They assumed He was somewhere else in the party. How far do we sometimes travel in life before we notice that Jesus is missing? How long do we go without praying, reflecting on our sins, or thanking God for all the blessings He gives us? How many people do

Jesus and the doctors of the Faith by Giuseppe Ribera (17th century)

you know who are moving away from God's grace through sin and just assume God is "cool" with everything they are doing? Like Mary and Joseph assuming that Jesus was still in the caravan, many times we assume that we are much closer to the Lord than we really are. Many times we willfully go against the Church's teaching and yet still think we are in God's grace. It takes a lot of strength and courage to really examine our actions, admit when we have drifted away from the way God calls us to live, and then turn back and rediscover Jesus. We reconnect with Jesus through the Sacrament of Reconciliation, prayer, and reading the Bible and the teachings of the Catholic Church. Basically, we find Jesus in His "Father's house" when we act according to His Church's teachings.

Mary and Joseph searched for Jesus for three days before finding Him. This is an important aspect of this mystery as it shows us that sometimes, even when we commit ourselves to finding Jesus in our lives, it can still be a long and difficult journey. We do not always instantly feel God's grace when we choose to reject sin and follow Jesus. Often people express frustration, depression, or anger with God because they do not feel His presence, although they are constantly looking for Him through prayer, fasting, and avoiding sin. But this mystery teaches us that we must not give up. We must constantly look for Jesus like a parent would look for a lost child. Mary and Joseph did not give up their search and neither should we. The Gospel describes that Mary and Joseph searched "in sorrow." Our path to Jesus might not be easy and there will probably be setbacks, dead ends, relapses, and disappointment. But this is one search that we must never call off because our very souls are at stake.

Let us meditate and pray for all of those who are moving away from God. We must pray especially for those whose pride has blinded them to God's truth. We must pray for those who twist the Church's teachings to justify sinful behavior. And we ask God for the strength to always turn towards Jesus' path and return to His Father's house when we stray. It does not matter how far off track we are, whether due to a single sin or to a lifetime of sinful behavior. We can always turn around and find God's mercy and love.

Intentions for this Mystery:
- For those living in sin, that they may return to God and receive His mercy and forgiveness.
- That we may have the strength to confess our sins in the Sacrament of Reconciliation.
- That we do not become discouraged in our search for the path God wants us to follow despite the challenges we may encounter.
- For teachers, that they are inspired by Jesus' teachings and pass them on to those they educate.
- For parents, that they continue to help steer their children towards God no matter how far they may have strayed from His path.

The Finding of the Savior in the Temple by William Holman Hunt (1860)

THE LUMINOUS MYSTERIES

Jesus' Baptism in the Jordan
The Miracle at Cana
The Proclamation of the Kingdom of Heaven and the Call to Conversion
The Transfiguration
The Institution of the Eucharist

The Luminous Mysteries focus on Jesus' public ministry and how He calls us to live for His Kingdom of Heaven. We focus on living with a truly converted heart, open to His grace.

THE FIRST LUMINOUS MYSTERY
JESUS' BAPTISM IN THE JORDAN

[13]*Then Jesus came from Galilee to John at the Jordan to be baptized by him.* [14]*John tried to prevent him, saying, "I need to be baptized by you, and yet you are coming to me?"*

[15]*Jesus said to him in reply, "Allow it now, for thus it is fitting for us to fulfill all righteousness." Then he allowed him.*

[16]*After Jesus was baptized, he came up from the water and behold, the heavens were opened [for him], and he saw the Spirit of God descending like a dove [and] coming upon him.* [17]*And a voice came from the heavens, saying, "This is my beloved Son, with whom I am well pleased."*
Matthew 3:13-17

Jesus' Baptism in the Jordan transforms a ritual of pouring water over one's head from representing a symbolic act of repentance to a real gift from the Holy Spirit that cleanses the soul of original sin. The central theme in this mystery is the washing away of sin as seen in the Sacrament of Baptism and the Sacrament of Reconciliation, and heard through John the Baptist's message of repentance. We prepare ourselves to fully receive God's grace when we approach Him in the sacraments with a truly repentant heart.

Think about how you take care of your teeth. You brush, rinse, and floss daily to keep them clean. However, every six months you also need to go to a dentist to have your mouth thoroughly inspected and cleaned by a professional. Seeing your dentist does not indicate bad oral health. Everyone needs regular brushing and checkups or else one's teeth will not stay their strongest. Skipping the daily brushing routine or the periodic checkups might lead to serious and sometimes irreversible dental problems.

Baptism of Christ by Francesco Albani (1600s)

What does oral hygiene have to do with the repentance of sins, except that many people probably consider a trip to the dentist as some sort of penance? Like brushing your teeth, prayer must be part of your daily routine to keep your soul healthy. Regular prayer is your time to reflect on all the ways you have lived God's will, and offer Him thanksgiving. Through prayer you also ask for strength and guidance to continue living a spiritually healthy life. Prayer serves as a little checkup to prevent sin from entering and decaying your soul. However, every so often you also need to see a professional to give your soul a thorough scrubbing away of sin. And that scrubbing is the Sacrament of Reconciliation.

Just as brushing alone is not enough to keep your teeth completely healthy, personal prayer alone is not enough to keep your soul at its best. You cannot wash away the effects of sin with only personal prayer. There are instances where your soul requires the help of a professional to fix the spiritual decay that may be attacking and spreading within you. When you receive the Sacrament of Reconciliation, the Holy Spirit restores your soul to a clean and healthy state.

This mystery should remind us of John the Baptist's message that we should "prepare the way of the Lord, make straight His paths" (Matthew 3:3). Let us remember to thoroughly repent, not just through our private prayers, but also by regularly receiving the Sacrament of Reconciliation. That way we clear our souls of everything that blocks us from fully receiving God's grace. Instead of seeing Confession as some sort of punishment, let us see it for what it really is — a gift. It is our chance to set things right, fix what is broken in our life, and build a stronger relationship with Jesus Christ. May we remember that it is through Confession that we return to that state of grace that we received at our Baptism. Let us make the effort to go to Confession regularly (the Church says at least once a year or immediately after committing a mortal sin) and live as true disciples of Jesus Christ.

Intentions for this Mystery:
- That we make time for prayer every day and ask God for strength and guidance.
- For those who have not received the Sacrament of Reconciliation in a long time, that they may find the courage to go and once again be united with God.
- For those addicted to drugs, alcohol, sex, and other vices, that they may come to know God's mercy.
- For all of us, that we remember that through our Baptism we made a promise to follow Jesus and obey His will.
- For those who are not baptized in the Church, that they may live morally and come to know God in their own way.

The Baptism of Jesus Christ
(author unknown)

THE SECOND LUMINOUS MYSTERY
THE MIRACLE AT CANA

¹On the third day there was a wedding in Cana in Galilee, and the mother of Jesus was there. ²Jesus and his disciples were also invited to the wedding. ³When the wine ran short, the mother of Jesus said to him, "They have no wine."

⁴[And] Jesus said to her, "Woman, how does your concern affect me? My hour has not yet come."

⁵His mother said to the servers, "Do whatever he tells you." ⁶Now there were six stone water jars there for Jewish ceremonial washings, each holding twenty to thirty gallons. ⁷Jesus told them, "Fill the jars with water." So they filled them to the brim. ⁸Then he told them, "Draw some out now and take it to the headwaiter." So they took it.

⁹And when the headwaiter tasted the water that had become wine, without knowing where it came from (although the servers who had drawn the water knew), the headwaiter called the bridegroom ¹⁰and said to him, "Everyone serves good wine first, and then when people have drunk freely, an inferior one; but you have kept the good wine until now."

¹¹Jesus did this as the beginning of his signs in Cana in Galilee and so revealed his glory, and his disciples began to believe in him.

John 2:1-11

At a wedding, Jesus turned water into wine in His first public miracle. This miracle started His ministry of healing the sick, giving sight to the blind, and giving mobility to the paralyzed. There are two main themes common to all the Gospels and they are Jesus' miracles and parables. Why are Jesus' miracles so critical to His ministry? And, if He could perform all these miraculous deeds, why did He not eliminate everyone's problems and hardships instantly? Why do we still have sick, blind, and paralyzed people today if it is so easy for the Lord to heal someone?

In order for Jesus' miracles to have meaning you must understand the reason behind them. He did not perform them for the sole purpose of making our lives easier. We cannot reduce Jesus to a mere genie who will grant us all our wishes. Instead, Jesus performed miracles to increase our faith and open us up to His truth. When Jesus gives sight to the blind He does a lot more than just heal one person. The miraculous act is a sign of His divinity and power so that many more will come to recognize Him as Christ our King and follow His teachings. We are like children where Jesus' miracles are a way of getting our attention so that we will be more receptive to His message. Jesus'

Wedding at Cana by Carl Bloch (1870s)

miracles are not only for the one He physically heals, but also for those who witness them so that their doubt transforms into faithfulness.

However, Jesus asks a lot of those He heals, whether it be physical or spiritual healing. He expects them to make a commitment to transform their lives, follow Him, live according to His will, and have faith that He will guide them to His heavenly kingdom. For example, consider Luke's Gospel where he talks of Jesus healing ten lepers. Of those ten only one came back to thank and praise Him, at which point Jesus said that his faith made him well. All those healed lepers eventually died, as we all do, so their physical healing was only temporary. But the one who returned to the Lord received more than temporary, physical healing. He received the gift of grace which is the true purpose of the miracle and more important than any physical healing. Ask yourself if you would have returned and thanked Jesus for His wonderful works. If you said yes, then ask yourself how many times you have thanked our Lord for the great miracle of a new day. What about for the miracle of friends? For the miracle of family?

Many times we are like the nine healed lepers who are given so much and yet we never return to thank the one who provides it all.

Do we pray for miracles for the right reasons? Do we ask for them to grow in our relationship with Jesus or do we ask for them to make our lives easier? We should remember that a miracle that only makes our lives easier is only temporary and will eventually fade away and be replaced by different challenges. But the gift of faith and God's grace is a miracle that will lead to eternal happiness. Let us remember that God always hears us even when our request for a miracle goes unanswered. God, in His infinite wisdom, knows that many of our requests only serve to make our lives easier and would not bring us any closer to Him and make us truly happy. Like a good parent, He knows when to tell us "no." Jesus did not come into this world to make our lives easier. Instead He came so that we may know Him and be with Him for all eternity in our next life. Let us pray this decade that Jesus' miracles heal our soul, increase our faith, and lead us closer to His love.

Intentions for this Mystery:
- That we see all the small miracles around us every day such as health, family, friends, and faith.
- For the spiritually lost or distressed, that Jesus' miracles help return them to their faith.
- For an increased understanding that miracles are for our spiritual benefit, not our earthly benefit.
- For those who are looking for a "quick fix" to their problems, that they instead show patience in Jesus' plans for them which lead to eternal happiness.
- That we learn from the miracles of others that Jesus is present in our world.

The Marriage at Cana by Marten de Vos (1597)

THE THIRD LUMINOUS MYSTERY
THE PROCLAMATION OF THE KINGDOM OF
HEAVEN AND THE CALL TO CONVERSION

[14]Jesus returned to Galilee in the power of the Spirit, and news of him spread throughout the whole region. [15]He taught in their synagogues and was praised by all. [16]He came to Nazareth, where he had grown up, and went according to his custom into the synagogue on the sabbath day.

He stood up to read [17]and was handed a scroll of the prophet Isaiah. He unrolled the scroll and found the passage where it was written: [18]"The Spirit of the Lord is upon me, because he has anointed me to bring glad tidings to the poor. He has sent me to proclaim liberty to captives and recovery of sight to the blind, to let the oppressed go free, [19]and to proclaim a year acceptable to the Lord."

[20]Rolling up the scroll, he handed it back to the attendant and sat down, and the eyes of all in the synagogue looked intently at him. [21]He said to them, "Today this scripture passage is fulfilled in your hearing."

Luke 4:14-21

We should remember that Jesus is the Word made Flesh who brought the power and glory of Heaven into this world. However, to celebrate in God's grace we must first approach Jesus with a humble heart open to conversion. By conversion, Jesus asks us to put away our worldly and sinful ways and truly embrace His teachings of goodness and mercy.

Early in His ministry, Jesus proclaimed the Word was fulfilled through Him. In a synagogue, Jesus read from the prophet Isaiah how "The Spirit of the Lord is upon me because He has anointed me." He followed up the reading saying how that passage was now fulfilled. As Christians who already believe in Jesus' divinity, this passage reads as a statement of fact and not a radical proclamation. However, this would have been difficult to hear for those gathered in the synagogue at that time. Instead of accepting Jesus as the Word made Flesh, they chased Him out of town.

Sermon on the Mount by Carl Bloch (1890)

We often chase Jesus away because we tell ourselves that what God asks of us does not make any sense, is too difficult, or is impossible to follow. It is often easier to find excuses and justifications to not accept God's truth. After all, the people who chased Jesus out of the temple reasoned that He was just the son of Joseph, the carpenter, and could not possibly be the Messiah. How often do we try to reason away God's truth, transform it, or revise it to suit our desire on how we want to live?

Jesus' ministry of healing and miracles showed the power and glory of God's kingdom. He gave sight to the blind, healed the sick, and restored movement to the paralyzed. Through His acts people came to believe and follow Him. Jesus did indeed bring the Kingdom of Heaven to the world, for wherever He traveled people felt the true presence of God. But it is amazing how quickly the people who followed Jesus abandoned Him. They praised Him one day only to call for His crucifixion the next. For many, Jesus was just a man who made their lives easier through physical healing. But they quickly abandoned Him when confronted with the difficult reality of following a man the ruling Roman authorities and Jewish leaders condemned to death.

Unfortunately, we carry on that legacy of human weakness of praising God when life is good and abandoning Him when life becomes difficult. How often do we become angry with God because something bad happens to us or we do not receive a desired outcome from our prayers? Life is not always easy or fair, but those with strong faith know that God is present when we need Him the most. Those other moments when we abandon God among hardship should serve as a reminder that we still need to work on our conversion for living for God's kingdom.

Intentions for this Mystery:
- For those who live only for this world, that they will start to live for God's Kingdom of Heaven.
- That we have the strength to convert our lives to Jesus' teachings and not try to bend His teachings to suit our desires.
- That we remain faithful even when it is difficult to live for Jesus' Kingdom of Heaven.
- For those who are persecuted for living according to Jesus' will, that they continue living as Jesus calls them.
- For those who hear the Word of God and yet reject it, that the Holy Spirit will open their hearts to God's truth.

Christ Teaching by William Brassey Hole
(20th century)

THE FOURTH LUMINOUS MYSTERY
THE TRANSFIGURATION

[27]*Truly I say to you, there are some standing here who will not taste death until they see the kingdom of God."* [28]*About eight days after he said this, he took Peter, John, and James and went up the mountain to pray.*

[29]*While he was praying his face changed in appearance and his clothing became dazzling white.* [30]*And behold, two men were conversing with him, Moses and Elijah,* [31]*who appeared in glory and spoke of his exodus that he was going to accomplish in Jerusalem.* [32]*Peter and his companions had been overcome by sleep, but becoming fully awake, they saw his glory and the two men standing with him.*

[33]*As they were about to part from him, Peter said to Jesus, "Master, it is good that we are here; let us make three tents, one for you, one for Moses, and one for Elijah." But he did not know what he was saying.*

[34]*While he was still speaking, a cloud came and cast a shadow over them, and they became frightened when they entered the cloud.* [35]*Then from the cloud came a voice that said, "This is my chosen Son; listen to him."* [36]*After the voice had spoken, Jesus was found alone. They fell silent and did not at that time tell anyone what they had seen.*

Luke 9:27-36

In this mystery, Jesus reveals himself as being God made man. This instance separates Jesus from the prophets of the Old Testament. He performed miracles and preached God's word, but so did the prophets. The Old Testament is full of accounts of people using God's grace to perform miracles such as Moses parting the Red Sea. But in the Transfiguration, Jesus shows that He is no mere prophet following God's will, but He is God's will, God's word, and God's truth in human form. This is why Moses and Elijah appeared next to Jesus as if God was differentiating Jesus' nature and mission from these earlier prophets.

God, creator of all that exists and ever will exist, the ultimate truth, our final judge, the Alpha and the Omega, humbled Himself and came into this world in a human form so that we may know Him personally. God desires all of us to live in His grace, and he became man through Jesus Christ so that we may better understand His ways. Our human minds cannot possibly understand God's infinite complexity and He knows that. So like an adult trying to explain a complex idea to a child, God revealed Himself in a very simple and direct way — by taking a form which people could see, hear, and touch through the man of Jesus Christ.

The Transfiguration by Lodovico Carracci (1594)

God gave the apostles a very direct command to listen to Jesus. And yet, after all they had seen and heard, they abandoned Jesus at His Crucifixion. Unfortunately, we continue to imitate the apostles' behavior when we disobey God by sinning. Imagine our arrogance to have received the word of God directly from Jesus and then deliberately disregard it because it conflicts with how we want to live or it seems too difficult. We might say we are followers of Christ, but when the time comes to humble ourselves to God's will and accept Jesus' teachings we often tell Him, "thanks, but no thanks." In the Transfiguration, God gave us a very simple and direct order on how we are to obtain grace -- listen to His son, Jesus Christ. And yet, each one of us can probably think of an instance when we refuse God's grace by sinning. We should take a moment to ask for God's mercy for those times we disobeyed Him.

God gave us an incredible gift through His son, Jesus Christ. No longer was God a thundering voice in the clouds or a burning bush, but instead was a living, breathing, and loving human being. We should remember the gift of the Catholic Church, starting with the first pope, St. Peter, who was there at the Transfiguration and later was personally appointed by Jesus to lead His people. God told us to listen to Jesus and therefore we must also listen and obey the teachings of His Church. We should pray for all of those who are wasting this precious gift by not listening or following God's will. We must pray for a world that seems to have gone out of its way not to listen to God's message.

God made Himself available to all of us through Jesus Christ. The question is, do we make ourselves available to God by listening to Him in prayer?

Intentions for this Mystery:
- That we thank God for taking human form so that we may forge a closer relationship with Him.
- That we ask for forgiveness for all those times when we have not followed Jesus' teachings.
- That we may make more time to listen to God in prayer and meditation.
- That we continue to search for the way God shows Himself to us in our lives.
- That we listen to God's prophets and messengers who preach God's truth.

The Transfiguration by William Brassey Hole (20th century)

THE FIFTH LUMINOUS MYSTERY
THE INSTITUTION OF THE EUCHARIST

[14]When the hour came, he took his place at table with the apostles. [15]He said to them, "I have eagerly desired to eat this Passover with you before I suffer, [16]for, I tell you, I shall not eat it [again] until there is fulfillment in the kingdom of God."

[17]Then he took a cup, gave thanks, and said, "Take this and share it among yourselves; [18]for I tell you [that] from this time on I shall not drink of the fruit of the vine until the kingdom of God comes." [19]Then he took the bread, said the blessing, broke it, and gave it to them, saying, "This is my body, which will be given for you; do this in memory of me." [20]And likewise the cup after they had eaten, saying, "This cup is the new covenant in my blood, which will be shed for you.
John 22:14-20

This mystery goes to the core of the Catholic faith -- that the bread and wine at Mass actually change into the Body and Blood of Jesus Christ. For Catholics, the Eucharist is not just a symbol, but is actually the very real presence of Jesus. The consecration of the bread and wine is no different from Jesus, in human form, walking through the doors of the church. And yet many of us receive Jesus regularly during Communion without appreciating the enormity of this gift.

The Last Supper by Leonardo DaVinci (1498)

The consecration requires one of the largest acts of faith from Catholics. After all, it is difficult to believe that a small wafer and some wine actually are Jesus Christ. There are many times when we receive the Eucharist on auto-pilot. Most of us probably wait in line, look around at other people and enjoy the music as if we were waiting for food in a cafeteria. But if Jesus, in His human form, walked through the door and spoke to us, He would have our complete attention. We would be reverent and attentive to everything He said. And yet, do we show that same reverence to His Body and Blood in the Eucharist? For most of us, no matter how hard we try, the answer would probably be no. If we really had even the faintest idea of the true nature of the Eucharist, we would not receive it so casually.

Since the Eucharist is the Body and Blood of Christ, we physically embrace Jesus every time we partake in the great, spiritual feast. We embrace Jesus by becoming sacred vessels of His Body and Blood. Think of the Eucharist as the fuel that empowers us to do God's will and face life's challenges. Without it, we are like a car with an empty gas tank — unable to do anything or go anywhere. The Eucharist is spiritual energy that we need to continue on the road to Heaven.

The word *communion* implies *community*. When we receive the Eucharist we are coming together as a community of believers in Jesus

Christ. Receiving the Eucharist is an affirmation in our belief and faith in Jesus' teachings and a public commitment to follow His will. It is this community of believers that is the core of the Catholic Church. We should pray that we all find strength through the Eucharist to show the world the power and love of Jesus Christ.

Intentions for this Mystery:
- That we show the Eucharist the respect it deserves and only receive it when we have a soul cleansed of all mortal sin.
- That we use the grace received in the Eucharist to show God's glory to the world.
- For those who do not attend Mass or receive the Eucharist, that they allow the Holy Spirit into their hearts to lead them back to Jesus' Church.
- For priests and Eucharistic ministers, that they find the energy to distribute the Body and Blood of Jesus to everyone in the community, particularly those who cannot attend Mass.
- For increased faith to believe that Jesus is truly present in the Eucharist.

The Last Supper by Palma il Vecchio (16th century)

THE SORROWFUL MYSTERIES

The Agony in the Garden
The Scourging at the Pillar
The Crowning of Thorns
The Carrying of the Cross
The Crucifixion

The Sorrowful Mysteries focus on Jesus' Passion and Crucifixion. We pray these mysteries for strength in the face of life's many hardships so that we can face them as Jesus did. May we endure and persevere through life's challenges with the faith that God will comfort us in Heaven.

THE FIRST SORROWFUL MYSTERY
THE AGONY IN THE GARDEN

³⁶Then Jesus came with them to a place called Gethsemane, and he said to his disciples, "Sit here while I go over there and pray." ³⁷He took along Peter and the two sons of Zebedee, and began to feel sorrow and distress. ³⁸Then he said to them, "My soul is sorrowful even to death. Remain here and keep watch with me."

³⁹He advanced a little and fell prostrate in prayer, saying, "My Father, if it is possible, let this cup pass from me; yet, not as I will, but as you will."

⁴⁰When he returned to his disciples he found them asleep. He said to Peter, "So you could not keep watch with me for one hour? ⁴¹Watch and pray that you may not undergo the test. The spirit is willing, but the flesh is weak."

⁴²Withdrawing a second time, he prayed again, "My Father, if it is not possible that this cup pass without my drinking it, your will be done!"

⁴³Then he returned once more and found them asleep, for they could not keep their eyes open. ⁴⁴He left them and withdrew again and prayed a third time, saying the same thing again. ⁴⁵Then he returned to his disciples and said to them, "Are you still sleeping and taking your rest? Behold, the hour is at hand when the Son of Man is to be handed over to sinners.

Matthew 26:36-45

This mystery revolves around prayer. We see Jesus facing His certain death. What does He do in that situation? Does He run and hide? Does He ask the apostles to fight and protect Him from those arresting Him? Does He complain endlessly and ask, "Why me?" No, instead He prays earnestly. According to the Gospel of Luke, Jesus prays so hard that He starts sweating blood. Ask yourself, have you ever prayed so hard for anything in your life? When you face large challenges, do you first turn to prayer and ask God for strength and guidance or do you try to run and hide? Or do you just throw out a quick, "God, help me!" without much effort or faith that God will actually do anything?

This rosary mystery really forces us to focus on the quality of our prayers. Do we earnestly lay our souls before God in prayer or do we just go through the words and motions? Many of us probably have other concerns on our mind when we pray, such as work, a television show or movie, finances, something someone said, or politics. Do we think about these things so that we can pray about them or are they distracting us from earnest prayer? When we pray are we like Jesus laying ourselves out before God or are we like the apostles in the garden —

An Angel Comforts Jesus by Carl Heinrich Bloch (19th century)

physically going through the motions and saying the words, but spiritually asleep?

In this mystery, we also see the dichotomy of Jesus being both fully human and fully God. He shows us very human emotions such as the fear of being tortured and killed and disappointment upon discovering His apostles sleeping instead of praying. He pleads with God that this terrible fate not befall Him. Fear and desperation are not exactly qualities we associate with God but ones we use to describe ourselves. And that is why we see Jesus in this very human state. If we saw the fully divine Jesus go to His death, fully at peace because He knew about His coming Resurrection, we would not be able to relate to or imitate Him. Seeing Jesus scared reminds us that fear is a normal human response when facing life's monumental obstacles and challenges. However, Jesus shows us that we cannot let those emotions impede us from doing God's will. We truly follow in Jesus' footsteps when we imitate His ways despite our human fears and doubts that make us want to do otherwise.

Let us try to pray earnestly with our whole heart, mind, and soul. We should set aside time every day to focus on prayer. Work, television, email, and web browsing can all wait for a few minutes. We all can increase our prayer intensity no matter where we are in our prayer life. That might mean trying to concentrate harder when praying the rosary, taking time out to say grace before a meal, or really focusing on prayers during Mass. Perhaps we can take the time to go to Adoration and really focus on building a stronger relationship with God. We should also pray for those who are feeling scared and trapped by life's obstacles. Whether they know it or not, they follow in Jesus' footsteps. God will give them strength and guidance just as He gave those gifts to Jesus in that lonely garden.

Intentions for this Mystery:
- For those who are going through difficulty in their lives, that they look to God for strength and endurance.
- For doctors and those who aid the sick, that God infuses them with strength to face all difficult cases.
- For those who do not pray often, that they will let the Holy Spirit into their hearts to inspire them to pray more.
- That we all make time in our lives for earnest prayer.
- That we do not avoid doing God's will out of fear of persecution or inconvenience.

The Grotto of the Agony by James Jacques Joseph Tissot (19th century)

THE SECOND SORROWFUL MYSTERY
THE SCOURGING AT THE PILLAR

[1]Then Pilate took Jesus and had him scourged. [2]And the soldiers wove a crown out of thorns and placed it on his head, and clothed him in a purple cloak, [3]and they came to him and said, "Hail, King of the Jews!" And they struck him repeatedly.

[4]Once more Pilate went out and said to them, "Look, I am bringing him out to you, so that you may know that I find no guilt in him." [5]So Jesus came out, wearing the crown of thorns and the purple cloak. And he said to them, "Behold, the man!"

[6]When the chief priests and the guards saw him they cried out, "Crucify him, crucify him!"

Pilate said to them, "Take him yourselves and crucify him. I find no guilt in him."

[7]The Jews answered, "We have a law, and according to that law he ought to die, because he made himself the Son of God."

John 19:1-7

Before condemning Jesus to death, the Roman authorities brutally whipped Him, as was the sentence for various crimes at that time. Scourging, like other forms of corporal punishment, helped cement Roman rule over their territories and deter anyone who dared to speak out against them. While innocent of any wrongdoing, Jesus suffered greatly for preaching God's truth, which undermined the Roman authorities.

Jesus' suffering is one of the harder aspects of His ministry to understand. It is easy to think of Jesus as the great teacher or the miracle worker. It is much more difficult to picture Him, God made man, as someone battered and bruised like any one of us. So why does Jesus choose this time of great suffering and hardship to show His humanity instead of His divine nature? After all, would not more people come to believe in Jesus and His teachings if He miraculously stopped the soldiers from harming Him? Would not a legion of angels descending from Heaven to defend Jesus turn even the most skeptical into believers?

Flagellazione di Cristo by Guercino (1657)

Jesus' suffering and death mimic His ministry. While we often wish that Jesus' message was one of easy answers and worldly comfort, we know that He instead laid before us a challenging path. He did not teach that no harm will ever come to those who believe in Him. In fact, He taught repeatedly that following His way would be fraught with inconveniences, hardship, and suffering. Unfortunately, our earthly kingdom and God's kingdom are largely incompatible and rapidly diverging from each other. And we find ourselves required to make a choice to live for one of these kingdoms. Jesus repeatedly said that those who remain faithful to His teachings, even in the midst of great suffering, will find comfort in Heaven for all eternity. Meanwhile, the world can only offer shallow and temporary comforts that eventually fade away.

Let us remember that life involves some sort of suffering one way or another. Jesus did not come into this world to end earthly suffering as exemplified by His scourging. We should pray that we gather the strength to follow Jesus' example whether that means enduring life's small hardships of living the faith or reconnecting with the Church after following a more worldly path. Remember, we never suffer alone since we share these burdens with each other, Jesus Christ, the Catholic Church, and the saints and angels.

Intentions for this Mystery:
- For those who turned away from the Church in hope of finding an easier life only to find more hardship. May their suffering be redemptive and make them stronger in their faith.
- For those who are actively persecuted throughout the world because of their love for Jesus Christ, that they continue to live faithfully.
- For the strength to endure any suffering we encounter while following Jesus' teachings.
- For the faith that all those who serve Jesus, even in great hardship, will find comfort in Heaven.
- For those who live solely for the comforts of this world at the expense of the eternal happiness of Heaven. May they open their hearts to the Holy Spirit to guide them back to God's grace.

The Flagellation of Christ by Caravaggio (1607)

THE THIRD SORROWFUL MYSTERY
THE CROWNING OF THORNS

¹⁶The soldiers led him away inside the palace, that is, the praetorium, and assembled the whole cohort. ¹⁷They clothed him in purple and, weaving a crown of thorns, placed it on him. ¹⁸They began to salute him with, "Hail, King of the Jews!" ¹⁹and kept striking his head with a reed and spitting upon him. They knelt before him in homage. ²⁰And when they had mocked him, they stripped him of the purple cloak, dressed him in his own clothes, and led him out to crucify him.
Mark 15:16-20

The Roman soldiers mocked Jesus by dressing Him in royal purple, crowning Him with thorns, and pretending to pay Him homage. Would the soldiers have acted so cavalier and arrogant if they truly understood who it was they were mocking? While we are not as brazen as those soldiers, we often mock Jesus by giving lip service to our faith. Instead of faithfully following Jesus, we too often dishonor Him by putting the fleeting treasures of this life in front of the treasures waiting for us in Heaven.

We are often very much like the Roman soldiers who pretended to pay Jesus homage. We may proclaim that we are Christian. We might recite prayers every night and go to Mass every Sunday. But do our actions show a deep devotion to Jesus Christ, our King and Savior? Will we follow Him even when times are difficult and our faith runs contrary to what society deems normal? Or do we dishonor Him by choosing a more worldly life? For example, do you follow beliefs

Christ Wearing the Crown of Thorns by Annibale Carracci (16th century)

that you know run contrary to the Church's teachings? Do you elevate the words and agendas of politicians above Jesus' teachings? Do you go to Confession without intending to truly turn away from your sins and live with a converted heart? There are so many ways where we proclaim Jesus as our king but our actions tell a different story. And while our transgressions may seem small and inconsequential, they are like the little thorns on the crown we offer to Jesus. When meditating on this mystery think about how sincerely your actions praise and honor Jesus. Do you practice and live the faith you profess or are you like the Roman soldiers who offer Jesus mock praise and homage?

For whose kingdom are you living? We too often live for this worldly kingdom and not for Jesus' Kingdom of Heaven. There are so many things that compete for our attention — money, power, possessions, and lust, just to name a few. We so easily crown the pleasures of the world as our king while honoring Jesus as an afterthought. But we must remember this verse from the Gospel of Matthew:

"No one can serve two masters. Either he will hate the one and love the other, or he will be devoted to the one and despise the other. You cannot serve both God and mammon (material wealth)" (Matthew 6:24).

As the verse says, we can only live for one kingdom. Unfortunately, since money and possessions are physical, quantifiable things it is often easier to live for them than it is to live for our treasures in Heaven. We see on television the comforts that wealth can bring us while the eternal joy of Heaven is something we take on faith. But you honor Jesus all the more when you take that difficult path of following Him instead of settling for the temporary treasures the world provides. When you pray this mystery ask yourself, what master are you serving? What type of crown do you offer Jesus Christ?

Intentions for this Mystery:
- For mercy for the times we put our worldly pursuits in front of our heavenly ones.
- That we can overcome our pride and acknowledge Jesus as our true Lord and Savior.
- That we remember to approach the sacraments with the utmost respect and reverence since they reflect Jesus' presence among us.
- For politicians and world leaders, that they govern with humility and let the Holy Spirit guide them in their decisions.
- That we approach the Sacrament of Reconciliation with a truly repentant heart to not repeat the same sins.

Jesus Mocked by William Brassey Hole (20th century)

THE FOURTH SORROWFUL MYSTERY
THE CARRYING OF THE CROSS

²⁶As they led him away they took hold of a certain Simon, a Cyrenian, who was coming in from the country; and after laying the cross on him, they made him carry it behind Jesus. ²⁷A large crowd of people followed Jesus, including many women who mourned and lamented him.

²⁸Jesus turned to them and said, "Daughters of Jerusalem, do not weep for me; weep instead for yourselves and for your children, ²⁹for indeed, the days are coming when people will say, 'Blessed are the barren, the wombs that never bore and the breasts that never nursed.' ³⁰At that time people will say to the mountains, 'Fall upon us!' and to the hills, 'Cover us!' ³¹for if these things are done when the wood is green what will happen when it is dry?"

Luke 23:26-31

This mystery encapsulates many of the Stations of the Cross. We see Jesus take up the cross, fall repeatedly, meet the mourning women, be stripped of His garments, and nailed to the cross. Like the other Sorrowful Mysteries, Jesus carrying His cross teaches us about the nature of suffering in that He calls us to love God and do His will despite any suffering we encounter in our lives.

Jesus falling while carrying the cross is significant since we dedicate three Stations of the Cross to it. Each time Jesus fell He got back up. But why did Jesus continue to get up and continue suffering under the heavy weight of the cross? Jesus must have known that each time He got up His situation was only going to get worse as He became more tired and beaten, and crucifixion was the only thing that awaited Him. Why did Jesus not just give up and die where He lay and avoid the ever increasing pain and torment? After all, Jesus' Resurrection would ultimately redeem us all. So why did it matter whether He died on

Christ Carrying the Cross by El Greco (1580)

the cross and not the moments before the crucifixion? What pushed Jesus to get back on His feet?

Jesus continued carrying the cross out of love for His Father and love for us. That love was greater than the physical pain He felt and it sustained Him throughout His torment. Jesus, while tired, bruised, and battered, demonstrated God's glory by showing that there was nothing the world could do to stop Him from living according to His Father's will. Likewise, Jesus calls us to follow God's will out of love, despite the suffering the world may impose on us. We know that part of loving someone is to make sacrifices at times. And while Jesus taking up His cross is an extreme example of this truth, this mystery reminds us that we all have the strength to dig deep and follow God regardless of the obstacles the world puts in front of us.

It is very common to question God's plan when we encounter suffering, we do not get what we want, or others do not treat us fairly. People often ask, "Why me?" "Why can't I find a job?" "Why can't I find a good spouse?" "Why did I get this illness?" The answer to all these questions lies within this mystery. Chances are we will all encounter some sort of suffering in this life. But when we endure the trials of this life by following Jesus' path, our faith tells us that we will eventually find comfort and relief in God's kingdom. Unfortunately, this is not the answer many of us want to hear. We want instant miracles. We want our problems to simply disappear. However, we do not see the big picture as God sees it. What we see as monumental suffering now ultimately amounts to nothing compared to the glory of Heaven that awaits us in the next life. In the end, finding eternal happiness in Heaven is all that really matters, not the momentary suffering and comforts in this world. Through God's grace we all have the strength to overcome any obstacles in this world, no matter how great, as Jesus did when He carried the cross.

Intentions for this Mystery:
- For those who live in sickness and sorrow, that they may continue to do God's will.
- For those who fell under the weight of the cross of sin, that they may find the strength to get back up and follow Jesus' path.
- That we have an awareness of the heavy crosses people carry and that we find the extra strength to help them.
- That we have faith that we will find comfort in Heaven when we continue to live by Jesus' teachings despite all our suffering in this life.
- For those who cannot find justice or fairness in this world, that they remain faithful knowing they will find it in Heaven.

The Procession Nearing Calvary by James Jacques Joseph Tissot (19th century)

THE FIFTH SORROWFUL MYSTERY
THE CRUCIFIXION

[16]*Then he handed him over to them to be crucified. So they took Jesus,* [17]*and carrying the cross himself he went out to what is called the Place of the Skull, in Hebrew, Golgotha.* [18]*There they crucified him, and with him two others, one on either side, with Jesus in the middle.* [19]*Pilate also had an inscription written and put on the cross. It read, "Jesus the Nazorean, the King of the Jews."*

[20]*Now many of the Jews read this inscription, because the place where Jesus was crucified was near the city; and it was written in Hebrew, Latin, and Greek.* [21]*So the chief priests of the Jews said to Pilate, "Do not write 'The King of the Jews,' but that he said, 'I am the King of the Jews.'"* [22]*Pilate answered, "What I have written, I have written."*

[25]*Standing by the cross of Jesus were his mother and his mother's sister, Mary the wife of Clopas, and Mary of Magdala.* [26]*When Jesus saw his mother and the disciple there whom he loved, he said to his mother, "Woman, behold, your son."* [27]*Then he said to the disciple, "Behold, your mother." And from that hour the disciple took her into his home.*

[28]*After this, aware that everything was now finished, in order that the scripture might be fulfilled, Jesus said, "I thirst."* [29]*There was a vessel filled with common wine. So they put a sponge soaked in wine on a sprig of hyssop and put it up to his mouth.* [30]*When Jesus had taken the wine, he said, "It is finished." And bowing his head, he handed over the spirit.*

John 19:16-22, 25-30

After suffering through the scourging, being mocked with a crown of thorns, and carrying a cross, Jesus died nailed to a tree alongside two criminals. According to the Gospel of Matthew, this puzzled people because Jesus saved others, but could not save Himself. Despite witnessing countless miracles, they wanted Jesus to perform one more miracle so that they would truly believe in Him. However, His largest miracle, conquering death and opening the gates of Heaven, was yet to come.

Jesus' Crucifixion is the ultimate example that we are all called to follow God's plan even in the face of great difficulty. Jesus, being the Son of God, could have easily put an end to His suffering any time He wanted. He was a man who walked on water, rose Lazarus from the dead, and healed countless people. Surely, coming down from the cross would have been an easy feat. And yet, He suffered and died horribly. Why? Because Jesus practiced what He preached. His entire ministry revolved around the principles of sacrifice, redemptive suffering, charity, forgiveness, and having faith in God's plan for us. And when the time came for His Crucifixion, Jesus did not ignore His teachings so that He could save His earthly body. As

Ancona Crucifiction by Titian (1558)

shown in the Fourth Sorrowful Mystery, Jesus did not come to save our physical bodies but instead cared about our eternal souls. When Jesus taught that we must "take up our cross" to gain salvation, He knew full well that those words also applied to Him. Therefore, as imitators of Christ, we cannot ignore or avoid God's will, even when we find ourselves in difficult situations.

Many people abandoned or mocked Jesus because He did not perform a miracle by coming down from the cross. Despite all they had seen and heard, in their minds Jesus came one miracle short for them to truly believe in Him. We often do the same thing when we approach Jesus in prayer. We want Him to do us one more favor. We tell Him we will truly live as one of His followers if He can do one more miracle for us. Like those at the foot of the cross, we often ask God for more while ignoring all that He has already done for us. We forget about the miracles of health, friends, family, and that we are alive and have an opportunity to live in God's grace.

We know that Jesus did in fact perform a great miracle when He died on the cross. By His Death and Resurrection He opened the gates of Heaven so that we all may find salvation through Him. Jesus' death gave us the miracle of a chance at eternal joy and happiness in His kingdom. All we have to do is come before Jesus in prayer and ask, with all humility, for Him to remember us. When the criminal who was crucified next to Jesus asked this, Jesus said that he would be with Him in paradise. Let us imitate the good criminal and not those who abandoned Jesus because they did not get the miracle they wanted. Instead, may we have faith in Jesus that He will provide for us all that we really need when we approach Him with a converted and humble heart.

Intentions for this Mystery:

- For those who feel wronged by others, that they look to forgive, not to punish.
- For criminals in our society, that they have the courage to ask for mercy, knowing that God forgives even the worst acts.
- That we show the humility to ask Jesus simply to remember us instead of continually asking Him to make our lives easier.
- That we may faithfully follow God's will knowing that everything Jesus taught applies to all of us.
- For those who hide their faith to avoid inconveniences or suffering, that they may come to understand the true joy of following Jesus even when it is difficult.

The Crucifixion by Simon Vouet (1622)

THE GLORIOUS MYSTERIES

The Resurrection
The Ascension
The Coming of the Holy Spirit
The Assumption of Mary
The Coronation of Mary

The Glorious Mysteries focus on Jesus taking His rightful place in Heaven and Mary being exulted as Queen of Heaven. With the guidance of Mary and the Holy Spirit may we live for our eventual resurrection into God's heavenly kingdom.

THE FIRST GLORIOUS MYSTERY
THE RESURRECTION

¹After the sabbath, as the first day of the week was dawning, Mary Magdalene and the other Mary came to see the tomb. ²And behold, there was a great earthquake; for an angel of the Lord descended from heaven, approached, rolled back the stone, and sat upon it. ³His appearance was like lightning and his clothing was white as snow. ⁴The guards were shaken with fear of him and became like dead men.

⁵Then the angel said to the women in reply, "Do not be afraid! I know that you are seeking Jesus the crucified. ⁶He is not here, for he has been raised just as he said. Come and see the place where he lay. ⁷Then go quickly and tell his disciples, 'He has been raised from the dead, and he is going before you to Galilee; there you will see him.' Behold, I have told you."

⁸Then they went away quickly from the tomb, fearful yet overjoyed, and ran to announce this to his disciples. ⁹And behold, Jesus met them on their way and greeted them. They approached, embraced his feet, and did him homage. ¹⁰Then Jesus said to them, "Do not be afraid. Go tell my brothers to go to Galilee, and there they will see me."

Matthew 28:1-10

Jesus rose from the dead showing us that our earthly death is not the end of our existence. We are more than just physical beings because we have souls meant to spend all eternity in Heaven. We should all remember that our lives in this world are only temporary. While we must make the most of what God has given us and live to the best of our abilities, we should remember that there is more to our existence than what we see and hear in this world.

If we are eternal beings, why do so many of us live as if our entire existence is bound to this world? The news constantly reports accounts of people acting however they wish, disregarding any of the harm they cause to others. We live in a culture where people live only for the present without regard for the consequences in this life, let alone the next one. As long as no one finds out about our sinful behavior, or punishes us, then we often feel that we did nothing wrong. Many times we falsely associate the lack of consequences with validation of our behavior. As

Resurrection of Christ by Noel Coypel (1700)

humans our faith is inherently weak. The Church tells us we will have to account for all our actions. And yet, we often do not have enough faith in Jesus' Resurrection and His Kingdom of Heaven to put away our sinful ways and fully embrace the life of grace to which Jesus calls us.

We can think of this world and our journey through life like travelers crossing a massive land bridge. The bridge was so long and wide that it seemed more like a continent than a crossing. There were signs posted everywhere on the bridge saying that there was a place more glorious than whatever we could imagine on the other side. And yet, so many people, not believing what lied ahead, built their entire kingdom on the bridge. They believed their castles and treasures were all they needed for true happiness. They ridiculed those who did not build their own castles but continued on their journey. The kings shouted from their golden towers, "You know there is nothing on the other end! Why don't you build yourself a castle and gather as many riches as you can so you find happiness like us?" However, one day the oceans rose and submerged the land bridge taking all the castles with it. The travelers, always packing lightly and moving with haste, made it to the other side safely while the kings drowned trying to hold on to as much treasure as possible.

The moral of the story is that those who only live for this world might not make it into God's Kingdom of Heaven. It is those who remember that this life is like a bridge and always make their focus the "other side" who will make it into Christ's kingdom. God gave us signs that we are eternal beings as seen in Jesus' Resurrection and through the teachings of the Catholic Church. But do we heed those signs? Ask yourself, are you more like the kings or the travelers from that story? How many times do you live only for this world despite the calling that Jesus desperately wants you to live for His Kingdom of Heaven? Through His Resurrection, Jesus showed the world that He calls us to new life after our earthly death. The question is, are you so bound by the treasures of this world that you do not make room in your heart for the treasures of Heaven?

Intentions for this Mystery:
- For those who live only for the world's riches, that they may see that there is more to their lives than what this world offers.
- That we remain spiritually nimble and not become bogged down by worldly money, comforts, possessions, and power.
- That we find joy in the fact that Jesus calls all of us to live with Him for all eternity in Heaven.
- That we do not fear the suffering of this world but have faith that we will find comfort in Heaven.
- That we continue to pray and present all our intentions, thanksgivings, and sorrows before God knowing that anything is possible through Him.

Angels Declaring Jesus is Risen by William Brassey Hole (20th century)

THE SECOND GLORIOUS MYSTERY
THE ASCENSION

[46]And he said to them, "Thus it is written that the Messiah would suffer and rise from the dead on the third day [47]and that repentance, for the forgiveness of sins, would be preached in his name to all the nations, beginning from Jerusalem. [48]You are witnesses of these things. [49]And [behold] I am sending the promise of my Father upon you; but stay in the city until you are clothed with power from on high."

[50]Then he led them [out] as far as Bethany, raised his hands, and blessed them. [51]As he blessed them he parted from them and was taken up to heaven. [52]They did him homage and then returned to Jerusalem with great joy, [53]and they were continually in the temple praising God.
Luke 24: 46-53

After rising from the dead, Jesus physically ascended into Heaven. We profess this every time we recite the "Apostles' Creed" at the beginning of the rosary — *He ascended into Heaven and is seated at the right hand of God the Father almighty; from there He will come again to judge the living and the dead.* We must remember that ultimately we will have to account for our thoughts, words, and actions in front of Jesus, who reigns in Heaven, and accept the consequences. However, the Church gives us tools that allow us to remain close to God and correct our faults before facing our final judgment.

"He will come again to judge the living and the dead." Most people fear the idea of final judgment. The word "judgment" conveys a trial, assessing guilt, and handing out punishment, none of which are very pleasant. When we are guilty (either legally or morally) many of us try to avoid admitting our faults and accepting the consequences. Judging often has a very negative connotation. We turn on those who point out our faults saying that they should not be so judgmental. We all would like to live an innocent, sinless, and virtuous life, but we often miss that mark. But in professing our inevitable judgment in the "Apostles' Creed" we remind ourselves that we need to work at becoming more Christ-like. Understanding that our actions have consequences motivates us to avoid committing sins. Furthermore, we should avoid sin because we realize that sin separates us from God's grace, the source of true happiness.

Ascension of Christ by Garofalo (1520)

The purpose of knowing of our coming judgment is not to scare or depress us. In fact, God does not want to punish any of us. He desires all of us to one day enter into His kingdom. And He provides tools to help us avoid a harsh judgment. The most obvious tool He gives us is the Sacrament of Reconciliation. This is our opportunity to set things straight with the Lord and remain in His grace. Confession is our way of doing small course corrections so that we can stay on the path that ultimately leads us into His Kingdom of Heaven. By routinely confessing our sins we face our shortcomings while they are still small and manageable. Without acknowledging our sins those small shortcomings can turn into major problems and separate us from God's grace, make our lives miserable, and possibly lose God's Kingdom of Heaven for all eternity.

Prayer is another tool at our disposal to live in God's grace. When we center our lives around God through prayer we cannot center it around sin. Earnest, heartfelt prayer provides us the knowledge and strength to avoid sin wherever it may present itself in our lives. The fact that we pray means that we acknowledge that Jesus sits at the right hand of the Father and hears our prayers. When we pray we focus, even if only for a short time, on the Lord and ask for His help, thank Him, and listen to how He calls us to live. In short, we ask for the strength to live for Jesus' kingdom and earn our place that He has prepared for us when He ascended into Heaven.

Intentions for this Mystery:
- For those who have died, that God may have mercy on their souls.
- For those who live in sin, that they turn toward God and ask for His forgiveness before their final judgment.
- For the souls in Purgatory, that God may quicken their purification so they can take their place in Heaven.
- That we have the strength to avoid sin so that we may quickly discover the joys and happiness of Heaven quickly after our earthly death.
- That we center our lives around prayer so that we may constantly live in God's grace.

The Ascension by James Jacques Joseph Tissot (19th century)

THE THIRD GLORIOUS MYSTERY
THE COMING OF THE HOLY SPIRIT

[16]And I will ask the Father, and he will give you another Advocate to be with you always, [17]the Spirit of truth, which the world cannot accept, because it neither sees nor knows it. But you know it, because it remains with you, and will be in you. [18]I will not leave you orphans; I will come to you. [19]In a little while the world will no longer see me, but you will see me, because I live and you will live. [20]On that day you will realize that I am in my Father and you are in me and I in you. [21]Whoever has my commandments and observes them is the one who loves me. And whoever loves me will be loved by my Father, and I will love him and reveal myself to him."

[22]Judas, not the Iscariot, said to him, "Master, [then] what happened that you will reveal yourself to us and not to the world?"

[23]Jesus answered and said to him, "Whoever loves me will keep my word, and my Father will love him, and we will come to him and make our dwelling with him. [24]Whoever does not love me does not keep my words; yet the word you hear is not mine but that of the Father who sent me.

[25]"I have told you this while I am with you. [26]The Advocate, the holy Spirit that the Father will send in my name—he will teach you everything and remind you of all that [I] told you."

John 14: 16-26

There are many gifts of the Holy Spirit. Unfortunately, we often treat the Holy Spirit as a genie who might grant us small favors. We often pray that the Holy Spirit will make a difficult situation simply go away. Like a little child we tell God that we will be good and believe in Him if He just helps us out this one time. That, of course, misses the entire point of the Holy Spirit.

The Holy Spirit does not come down to magically change the world to make our lives easier. As much as we may wish it, the Holy Spirit does not pave over all of life's challenges so that we may live any way we wish. After all, the world in which the apostles lived did not magically change on Pentecost. The people who wished them harm were still out there. Those who crucified Jesus did not vanish. The apostles knew Jesus' teachings but needed that little "kick" from the Holy Spirit to proclaim those teachings to the world.

The Outpouring of the Holy Spirit by Anthonis von Dyck (1620)

One of the most significant gifts of the Holy Spirit is courage to do God's will. The Holy Spirit gave the apostles the courage to go out and proclaim God's Word. And they boldly preached it even when they were ridiculed, persecuted, and martyred. The Holy Spirit provided them the strength and courage to teach God's love in a very hostile world.

Thousands of years later, we still find ourselves in a world hostile to God's truth. The Church is under attack from all sides whether it be other religions, politicians, or popular culture. But like the apostles we too receive courage from the Holy Spirit to live according to God's will. There are times when we do the right thing even when we know doing something different would be a lot easier. Those are the times when we listen to the Holy Spirit's guidance and live as one of God's children. When we resolve to live according to God's will and choose good over evil, the Holy Spirit will give us that little push in the right direction as He did with the apostles.

There are many other gifts of the Holy Spirit. However, courage to do God's will is one of the gifts we often overlook. Let us pray and reflect that the Holy Spirit will give us the courage to do God's will even if it makes our earthly lives more difficult. The next time we think about taking an easy way out of a difficult situation, let us look to the Holy Spirit to lead us back to what is right and face whatever consequences come our way.

Remember, God never gives us challenges we cannot handle. At times life's difficulties may seem insurmountable, but God gives us everything we need to ultimately triumph. He gives us the Holy Spirit, the sacraments, the Magisterium of the Catholic Church, and an army of saints and angels to guide us. With all of these resources at our disposal there is nothing this world can throw at us that we cannot overcome.

Intentions for this Mystery:
- That we have an open heart and mind and listen to how the Holy Spirit guides us.
- That we look to the Holy Spirit for strength to do God's will.
- That we find the courage to live our faith proudly and publicly.
- That the Holy Spirit gives us strength to mend any broken relationships in our lives.
- That we use all of our God-given gifts and talents to spread the teachings and love of Jesus Christ.

Pentecôte by Jean II Restout (1732)

THE FOURTH GLORIOUS MYSTERY
THE ASSUMPTION OF MARY

[45]Blessed are you who believed that what was spoken to you by the Lord would be fulfilled."

[46]And Mary said: "My soul proclaims the greatness of the Lord; [47]my spirit rejoices in God my savior. [48]For he has looked upon his handmaid's lowliness; behold, from now on will all ages call me blessed."
Luke 1:45-48

Having accepted God's plan for her in the Annunciation, God honored Mary by assuming her, body and soul, into His kingdom. However, her work was far from over as she now takes the role of our guide and spiritual mentor. She is always trying to bring us closer to her son, Jesus Christ. She has a difficult challenge since she needs to not only fight the forces of evil, but also fight against our own human weaknesses to live as one of God's children.

Mary has appeared to many people over the centuries and reiterated the ways we can live in God's grace and ultimately live in His Kingdom of Heaven. Her messages can be summarized in five core behaviors:

Assumption of Mary by Guido Reni (1642)

• **Pray:** How can you have a meaningful relationship with God unless you talk to Him? It does not matter whether you recite prayers, meditate, or just have a free-form prayer session. You need to talk to God and, more importantly, listen to what He tells you.

• **Read the Bible:** How can you love God if you do not know Him and His Church? Read the Bible, the Catechism, and the writings of saints and scholars. Know your faith so that you can live it with every thought, word, and action.

• **Fast:** The key is to detach yourself from the materialistic bonds of this world and leave room in your soul for God's grace. More than just a detox for the body, fasting is a powerful way of remembering all that God gives us. Compared to other periods of history, we live in a fairly comfortable world. Nearly everything we want is found with a trip to the store or a few clicks on a computer. Fasting puts all our wants into perspective and makes us remember that what will make us truly happy is something we cannot find in a store or online. When we fast, we remember the temporary nature of this world and that the only permanence is found through God.

• **Confess:** You need to free yourself from the bonds of sin by receiving absolution. Like a shower for your soul, the Sacrament of Reconciliation cleans the damage sin inflicts on you and strengthens your resolve to stay in a state of grace.

- **Receive the Eucharist:** You need to receive Jesus' Body and Blood regularly because it is your spiritual fuel that will give you the strength and resolve to do God's will.

Remember these as the five "R's" of Christian living – Recite, Read, Refrain, Repent, and Receive. When you wake up in the morning, just recite these five words so that they will be on your mind throughout the day.

What Mary asks of us is not terribly difficult. She asks us to recognize God in our lives through prayer and to act according to His will. Taking the time to listen to Mary and following her guidance will lead to something far greater than anything in this world — God's kingdom. So, when we pray this mystery we should ask ourselves, "Are we listening to our Heavenly Mother?"

Intentions for this Mystery:
- That we look to Mary to guide us into God's grace.
- That we look to Mary for help against the wickedness and snares of Satan.
- That we have the strength to fast and abstain from worldly comforts so that we can fill our hearts with Jesus' love.
- That we have the strength to receive the Sacrament of Reconciliation so that we remain close to God.
- That we learn from Mary and the saints how to obtain our place in God's heavenly kingdom.

L' elezione della Vergine by Francesco Botticini (15th century)

THE FIFTH GLORIOUS MYSTERY
THE CORONATION OF MARY

[49]"The Mighty One has done great things for me, and holy is his name. [50]His mercy is from age to age to those who fear him. [51]He has shown might with his arm, dispersed the arrogant of mind and heart. [52]He has thrown down the rulers from their thrones but lifted up the lowly. [53]The hungry he has filled with good things; the rich he has sent away empty. [54]He has helped Israel his servant, remembering his mercy, [55]according to his promise to our fathers, to Abraham and to his descendants forever."
Luke 1:49-55

In this mystery we see Mary awarded the honor of Queen of Heaven for having wholeheartedly accepted God's call. Early Christians gave Mary this title long before the Catholic Church officially expressed it. In Hebrew tradition, the mother of a king is considered the queen. And since Jesus is King of Heaven, it follows that Mary is Queen of Heaven. This is Her rightful place for having faith in God's plan in the Annunciation, spreading God's joy in the Visitation, giving birth to Jesus, King of the World, and ultimately accepting the sorrow of His Crucifixion and death. Mary is now in Heaven and amplifies and purifies our prayers and presents our needs to her son, Jesus Christ. Mary's coronation gives her many titles such as the Queen of Peace, Queen of Angels, Queen of Saints, and Queen of the Rosary.

Mary is the Queen of Peace. Typically, we think of peace as a world without war and conflict. And while that is a lofty goal and something worth praying for, Mary and the saints want us to dig deeper. We cannot have peace in this world unless we have an inner peace with God. She wants us to work towards this internal peace by reconciling our ways with God's ways. She calls us to align ourselves with the teachings of Jesus Christ as handed to us through the Church. This means putting aside worldly desires of money, power, fame, popularity, and anything else that might distract us from doing God's will. Mary knows that we cannot have real peace as long

Coronation of the Virgin by Diego Velazquez (1645)

as there is conflict in our hearts between our love for Jesus and our love for worldly comforts.

Mary is the Queen of Angels. We must remember the angels in our prayers, particularly our guardian angels who protect us. While we may not be aware of it, angels fight against the forces of evil every day to protect our souls from Satan and his minions. Mary understands the precious gift of being in God's grace and desires all of us to remain in communion with Jesus Christ. She directs the angels to fight for us because She does not want anyone to lose the gift of grace, especially for the momentary and trivial pleasures of this world.

Mary is certainly the Queen of the Rosary. The rosary is our way of communicating with God. We pray it remembering all the sorrows, joys, and glories of Jesus Christ. When we pray the Joyful Mysteries we pray for the strength to accept God's plan for us as Mary did. In the Luminous Mysteries we pray for the strength to live according to Jesus' teachings. When we pray the Sorrowful Mysteries we pray for the strength to remain faithful in the face of great suffering. And in the Glorious Mysteries we pray for the awareness and faith to live for our eventual resurrection into God's kingdom and stand before Jesus Christ. Mary gives us a great gift in the rosary because we can use it to reflect on all dimensions of our faith. It reminds us to thank God for all He gives us, ask for forgiveness of our sins, and ask Him for strength to live according to His truth.

Intentions for this Mystery:
- For our guardian angels who constantly protect us from harm.
- That we learn from the examples of the saints how to live in God's grace.
- For aid and protection of those most susceptible to Satan's false promises.
- That we may find the strength to live in peaceful accordance with Jesus' Church.
- That we find the time to earnestly pray and forge a deeper relationship with God, especially by praying the rosary.

Coronación de la Virgen by Vicente Castelló
(17th century)

Use this page to guide you in your prayers if you do not have a rosary available.

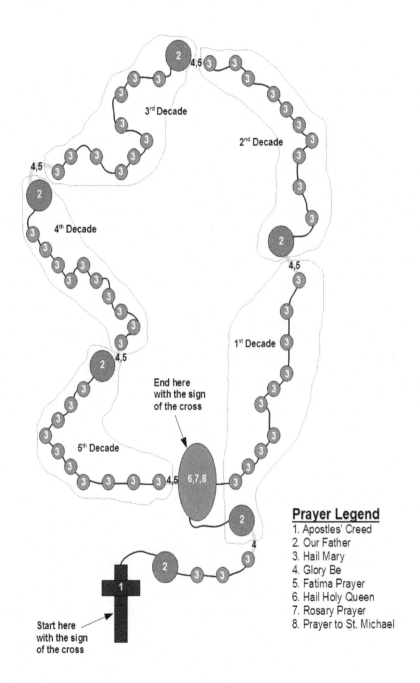

3rd Decade

2nd Decade

4th Decade

1st Decade

End here
with the sign
of the cross

5th Decade

6,7,8

Start here
with the sign
of the cross

Prayer Legend
1. Apostles' Creed
2. Our Father
3. Hail Mary
4. Glory Be
5. Fatima Prayer
6. Hail Holy Queen
7. Rosary Prayer
8. Prayer to St. Michael

ABOUT THE AUTHOR

Brent Villalobos created www.rosarymeds.com, a website dedicated to helping people better understand the rosary and integrate it into their lives. The site makes connections between the rosary and readings from the Bible as well as what the rosary can teach us about current events. The articles on that website formed the basis for this book. Brent is a software engineer who took an interest in web technologies, particularly blogging, in 2008 when he participated in *The 30 Day Challenge* (www.challenge.co). And so RosaryMeds and "The Rosary for the Rest of Us" became a great merger of his technical interests, software skills, and spiritual life.

Made in the USA
Monee, IL
23 November 2021

82866356R00056